# BLACK FATHERS IN CONTEMPORARY AMERICAN SOCIETY

# BLACK FATHERS IN CONTEMPORARY AMERICAN SOCIETY

## Strengths, Weaknesses, and Strategies for Change

OBIE CLAYTON

RONALD B. MINCY

DAVID BLANKENHORN

EDITORS

RUSSELL SAGE FOUNDATION / NEW YORK

# The Russell Sage Foundation

The Russell Sage Foundation, one of the oldest of America's general purpose foundations, was established in 1907 by Mrs. Margaret Olivia Sage for "the improvement of social and living conditions in the United States." The Foundation seeks to fulfill this mandate by fostering the development and dissemination of knowledge about the country's political, social, and economic problems. While the Foundation endeavors to assure the accuracy and objectivity of each book it publishes, the conclusions and interpretations in Russell Sage Foundation publications are those of the authors and not of the Foundation, its Trustees, or its staff. Publication by Russell Sage, therefore, does not imply Foundation endorsement.

**Library of Congress Cataloging-in-Publication Data**

Black fathers in contemporary American society: strengths, weaknesses, and strategies for change / Obie Clayton, Ronald B. Mincy, David Blankenhorn, editors.
    p. cm.
  Includes bibliographical references and index.
  ISBN 0-87154-161-0
  1. African American fathers. 2. African American men—Family relationships. 3. African American families. I. Clayton, Obie, 1954- II. Mincy, Ronald B. III. Blankenhorn, David.

HQ756 B55 2003
306.874'2'08996073—dc21

2002036741

The paper used in this publication meets the minimum requirements of American National Standard for Information Sciences–Permanence of Paper for Printed Library Materials. ANSI Z39.48-1992.

Text design by Suzanne Nichols

RUSSELL SAGE FOUNDATION
112 East 64th Street, New York, New York 10021
10 9 8 7 6 5 4 3 2 1

# CONTENTS

# CONTRIBUTORS

OBIE CLAYTON is professor and chair of the Department of Sociology at Morehouse College and executive director of the Morehouse Research Institute.

RONALD B. MINCY is the Maurice V. Russell Professor of Social Policy and Social Work Practice at the School of Social Work, Columbia University.

DAVID BLANKENHORN is president of the Institute for American Values.

ENOLA G. AIRD is an affiliate scholar and director of the Motherhod Project at the Institute for American Values, New York.

LAWRENCE D. BOBO is Norman Tishman and Charles M. Diker Professor of Sociology and African American Studies at Harvard University.

MAGGIE GALLAGHER is an affiliate scholar at the Institute for American Values.

WADE F. HORN is Assistant Secretary for Children and Families in the U.S. Department of Health and Human Resources. He previously served as president of the National Fatherhood Initiative, as director of Outpatient Psychological Services at the Children's Hospital National Medical Center in Washington, D.C., and on the faculty of George Washington University.

JOAN W. MOORE is distinguished professor emerita at the University of Wisconsin, Milwaukee.

BARBARA MORRISON-RODRIGUEZ is president and CEO of BMR Consulting, LLC, in Tampa, Florida. At the time the chapter was written, she was the I. DeQuincy Newman Professor of Social Work at the University of South Carolina.

STEVEN L. NOCK is professor of sociology at the University of Virginia.

HILLARD POUNCY is an independent scholar.

WORNIE L. REED is professor of sociology and urban studies at Cleveland State University.

WILLIAM JULIUS WILSON is the Lewis P. and Linda L. Geyser University Professor and Director of the Joblessness and Urban Poverty Research Program at Harvard University.

# FOREWORD

The family is arguably the core institution of human social existence. For this reason, those interested in understanding the conditions, status, and prospects of any ethnic-racial group typically make the family a central topic of concern. Social scientific efforts to assess the circumstances of African Americans have long focused a close analytical eye on the black family. A large and varied literature has developed through the years, spanning major scholarly treatises, policy papers, and other analyses, as well as bitter polemics and baneful jeremiads. But as economic structures, social policies, and social norms continue to change, we will need even more careful assessments of how these families are faring, especially the families of those most disadvantaged in society.

Some crucial continuities in the dynamics of African American families have emerged in previous research. Indeed, the most important of these key themes can be traced back to the earliest scholarship in the area and are still relevant today. The first serious investigation of the black family was W. E. B. Du Bois's pioneering sociological work *The Philadelphia Negro*, first published in 1899. In his meticulous study of blacks in the city's Seventh Ward, Du Bois identified what he termed "the early breaking up of family life" among blacks as a serious problem (Du Bois 1899/1996, 66–67). One finds in DuBois's work three themes of enduring importance for research on black family life: the greater fragility of the black family unit, coming out of the traumatic and oppressive experience of slavery; the importance of economic resources both to whether men and women decide to enter into marriage and to the sustenance of stable family units; and a call upon blacks, most often in the form of a value judgment, to establish stronger, healthier family ties and norms. Here as always, the normative benchmark has been that of the nuclear family, a stable husband-wife unit nurturing and raising their own biological offspring. Detailing and enlarging upon these themes continues to play a large part in discussions of black families, marriage patterns, and relations between black men and women.

It is something of an understatement to say that controversy has been the most prominent feature of research on black families. In their ferocity, the public and scholarly debates have often drawn attention away from the important practical matters of black family dynamics that require our most urgent attention and concern. In the 1930s and 1940s the critical dispute was over whether there were any important African cultural retentions that needed to play a role in understanding black family life. In the 1960s and 1970s, of course, there was the highly divisive and ultimately counterproductive furor over the "Moynihan Report" and its depiction of black families as dysfunctional, matriarchal, and caught in a "tangle of pathology." And more recently we have seen an equally caustic set of disputes around sex, sexuality, and marriage issues between black men and women—a set of tensions perhaps most vividly and distressingly epitomized by the Clarence Thomas–Anita Hill controversy during the congressional hearings on his Supreme Court nomination.

Separating the valuable wheat of good research and meaningful theory on African American families from the abundant chaff of contention and acrimony is no easy task. However, it is imperative that we do so, precisely because our understanding cannot be complete without a thoroughgoing analysis of so fundamentally important an institution as the family. Moreover, it is surely fair to say that African Americans can fully realize the American Dream only when their family units are whole, healthy, and vibrant, however those units may be configured.

In all of the research and debate, surprisingly little attention has been dedicated to the part played by black fathers. In this critically important volume, Obie Clayton, Ron Mincy, and David Blankenhorn set out to understand black fathers, both their indispensable roles and obligations and the challenges and obstacles they face in contemporary American society. The research reported in this volume and the ways in which the issues are addressed cut straight through the old polemics and lines of contention. The work here provides serious and trenchant answers to the question of what types of contributions black fathers can and do make in families. This volume's contributors address how much black fathers matter to their children, and why they matter. They also propose what both social policy and black families and communities now need to do to strengthen the contributions of black fathers to their children, families, and communities.

There are three reasons to heed the lessons of this volume. First, as the sociologist Obie Clayton and his colleagues emphasize—in a manner immediately reminiscent of the observations of Du Bois a century ago—there is plenty of evidence of the fragility of black families. As other chapters in this volume point out, this fragility has become apparent at a time when the evidence on the advantages—social, psychological, and material—of two-parent families becomes more and more compelling. Yet, as the editors stress, we should not assume that we are fated to witness an ever-rising percentage of black children being raised in single-parent, female-headed households. As recent trends suggest, when a robust, expanding economy and social policy support family formation, a previously unabated upward trend in single-parent female headship can be halted for a time.

A second ground for focusing intensively on the roles of fathers is that a large fraction of black families, particularly those with children, remain in economic marginally conditions. Indeed, a major study by the Children's Defense Fund reports a distressing rise in the number of black children living in conditions of extreme poverty. Falling into poverty is plainly much more likely for children who do not have the regular support of both a mother and a father. As the chapters in this volume point out, two-parent households are not only better able to adapt to economic dislocations but are in a far better position to accumulate wealth. The critically important sociological research of Melvin Oliver and Thomas Shapiro has made clear the powerful role played by wealth—not merely employment and earnings—in sustaining a family's quality of life over the long haul.

And third, we know that families are essential to the nurturance and socialization of children. As the chapters in this volume make clear, two parents usually have more material resources and psychological resources, make unique and specialized contributions to the family, and have more time to devote to preparing their children for the future than could ever be provided by a lone parent or by other caregivers with uncertain obligations and commitments to those children (absent, of course, great financial affluence). Yet, as the position of black men in the economy has weakened, we see that a greater fraction of them resist entry into marriage. Women in general, and especially black women in low-income circumstances, are with some justification wary of potential mates who lack a solid economic foundation and future. One result of this confluence of circumstances has been both mounting evidence of friction and suspicion between black men and women and a rising number of children born out of wedlock.

But it is imperative that black fathers, whether custodial or noncustodial, be a substantial and consistent presence in the lives of their children. There is little doubt that the frayed bonds between black fathers and their offspring are largely the result of factors that have profoundly marginalized vast numbers of low-skilled black men: the economy, social policies, and an at-best indifferent public. These factors are heavily implicated in the risk of living in poverty faced by many black children today. But whatever the source, such frayed bonds of family and parenthood are also one reason young blacks, especially young black men in poor communities, are more likely to be swept up into the criminal justice system.

To be sure, a convincing and growing body of research shows that there is a complex but understandable relationship between economic conditions, family structure, and the likelihood that children will drift toward juvenile delinquency and crime. Steady economic hardship and marginality weakens the likelihood that men and women will marry and form stable family units. When the bonds and resources of the two-parent family unit are weakened—and those of the surrounding community are thus also weakened—the capacity to socialize and closely supervise children wanes as well. Children without close parental supervision, especially perhaps teenage males, are susceptible to the lure of the street, or what sociologist Mary Pattillo has called "the ghetto trance." These circumstances, which characterize all too many low-income black communities, open the door to involvement in risky behavior, juvenile delinquency, and crime.

A focus on the role of fathers does not diminish or dismiss the roles of mothers. Nor does it place a prior or special premium on the needs of men and fathers. Rather, it acknowledges that research on black families has developed a great imbalance. It has been easier, for understandable reasons, to focus on the circumstances and behaviors of those most routinely in a household (mothers and children) or those for whom social policy (for instance, TANF, formerly AFDC) has made more explicit provision. Fathers must be brought back into the picture, especially in a social context in which a huge absolute percentage of black families are single-parent, female-headed households and in which African Americans, especially young black men, face an alarmingly high lifetime probability of incarceration. Both the research and policymaking communities should sift carefully through this important set of studies, which make a vital contribution to filling the enormous gap in our thinking about African American fathers and families.

LAWRENCE D. BOBO

## REFERENCES

Dillion, Sam. 2003. "Report Finds Deep Poverty Is On the Rise." *The New York Times,* Wednesday, April 30, 2003.

Du Bois, W. E. B. 1996[1899]. *The Philadelphia Negro: A Social Study.* Philadelphia, Pa.: University of Pennsylvania Press.

Oliver, Melvin L. and Thomas M. Shapiro. 1995. *Black Wealth/White Wealth: A New Perspective on Racial Inequality.* New York: Routledge.

Pattillo-McCoy, Mary. 1999. *Black Picket Fences: Privilege and Peril Among the Black Middle Class.* Chicago: University of Chicago Press.

# ACKNOWLEDGMENTS

This book largely stems from conversations on the future of the family that began among the editors in 1996 and 1997. Each editor was in agreement that responsible fatherhood should be given more nonpartisan attention. Further, we saw the necessity of having a public forum where both research and policy issues concerning the family could be discussed. With this backdrop, we began planning a conference on the state of fatherhood in black America, and it soon became obvious that father absence was more than a black problem. We took our ideas to several foundations and secured funding for the project. To this end, we are grateful to the Ford Foundation, the Achelis and Bodman Foundations, the Russell Sage Foundation and the Annie E. Casey Foundation for their generous support, which made the conference and this volume possible. We would like to give special acknowledgments to Robert Curvin, Susan Berressord and Melvin Oliver of the Ford Foundation for their role in supporting initiatives around families and fathers.

In addition to the foundations named above, we would like to thank the staff of the Institute for American Values, especially Josephine Abbatiello for her dedication and commitment to the project. Ms. Abbatiello was responsible for staying in contact with the authors and putting the manuscript in electronic form. Ms. Charity Navarrete was also a valuable asset to the project, providing the fiscal accounting that was necessary to a project of this scale. Ms. Iretha Stoney of the Morehouse Research Institute was the main conference planner and had the awesome task of interfacing with over fifty participants and two hundred attendees. She is to be commended for her professionalism and commitment.

This volume is dedicated to Mrs. Annie S. Clayton, a mother who embodies the importance of family, to the memory of Obie Clayton Sr. (1911–1999), and to the memory of all the good fathers who came before and on whose shoulders we stand.

OBIE CLAYTON
RONALD B. MINCY
DAVID BLANKENHORN

# INTRODUCTION

## DAVID BLANKENHORN AND OBIE CLAYTON

In November of 1998, Morehouse College and the Institute for American values convened a conference on the state of African American fathers. Presenters at that conference included William Julius Wilson, Steven Nock, Glenn Loury, Elijah Anderson, and Ron Mincy, to name but a few. All of these scholars have done research in the area of the African American family and their work is highly respected both within the academy and among the general public. One statement that stood out particularly strongly was made by William Raspberry, the Pulitzer Prize–winning columnist, when he pondered aloud the question we had asked him to address himself to: "Are black fathers necessary?" His answer:

> Are black fathers necessary? You know, I'm old and I'm tired, and there are some things I just don't want to debate anymore. One of them is whether African American children need fathers. Another is whether marriage matters. Does marriage matter? You bet it does. Are black fathers necessary? Damn straight we are. (Raspberry 1998)

Raspberry's statement forced those in attendance to think about the problems facing the family in contemporary society and, perhaps more important, raised the question: What is the role of the father in the lives of their children? For anyone concerned about the well-being of our nation's children, is any demographic fact more disturbing, more demanding of our collective attention, than the fact that the great majority of African American children do not live with their fathers? Similarly, is any demographic fact more hopeful, or more demanding of our collective encouragement, than the fact the proportion of African American children living with both their biological, married parents, although still quite low, has risen significantly since 1995?

In some respects, this entire volume is about those two facts. What do they mean for black children? For all children? For the possibility

1

of improved relationships between black men and black women? For U.S. public policy? For the possibility of racial justice, healing, and reconciliation? For our society as a whole? These are questions of great importance, and to their credit, the diverse contributors to this volume—blacks and whites, women and men, conservatives and liberals, and scholars from a variety of disciplines and backgrounds—treat them with the intellectual and moral seriousness that such questions deserve, but generally have not received in academic and public discussions.

Many of the chapters in this volume address the two major changes in family formation identified above. Recent positive changes are not large or definitive, but they are certainly suggestive. And if they continue, they will change the lives of millions of U.S. children and families for the better. Already these changes, particularly with respect to the black family, have demonstrated quite clearly that scholars and other leaders who have long insisted that nothing can be done to change trends in family structure are wrong. In 1997, Donna L. Franklin echoed a widely held view when she stated: "Policy makers will have more of an impact on the lives of poor and African American children when they accept the irreversibility of high levels of non-marriage of their mothers as a starting point for thinking about changes in public policy" (Franklin 1997, 219). Yet recent positive demographic trends in black (and, more broadly, U.S.) family structure suggest that there is nothing "irreversible" about the trends of father absence and family fragmentation.

The reintegration of nurturing black fathers into the lives of their children is the primary focus of the chapters that follow, but the reader will also quickly see several other themes in these papers: more paternity identification, more child support payments from nonresidential fathers, and noncustodial fathers who have better parenting and job skills and are visiting their children more often. If and when these current trends continue and becomes more firmly established in the years ahead, many other good results—including reductions in child poverty, greater asset accumulation for black families, reduced levels of crime, and reductions in domestic violence—are likely to follow.

This book is organized in three major parts. Part I (chapters 1 and 2) offers explanations for the declines in marriage within the African American family from several theoretical perspectives. In chapter 1, William Julius Wilson provides the necessary context for us to understand many of the problems facing inner-city families and fathers. Wilson asserts that marriage among many inner-city males is not felt by them to be an option: "[B]ecause of their experiences with extreme economic marginality, they tend to doubt that they can achieve approved societal goals." Wilson views declines in marriage rates among blacks as a direct function of restricted opportunities. In essence, he sees structural conditions in the inner city as the primary cause for declines in the marriage rates.

Chapter 2, by Steven Nock, looks at the benefits of marriage and suggests that men who marry and have children are better off economically and socially and have longer life expectancies than their unmarried counterparts.

Each of the chapters in part II (chapters 3, 4, and 5) looks at a different aspect of marriage from an economic perspective. All emphasize the significance of marriage as in part a wealth-building institution. Married people earn, invest, and save more than unmarried people. In chapter 3, Ronald Mincy and Hillard Pouncy articulate a thesis that is unique in the literature; from their data they infer that the inability of many black males to achieve economic parity may lie in the fact that welfare supports goes disproportionately to black mothers and ignores black fathers. This may in turn discourage marriage among young unwed parents.

Chapter 4, by Maggie Gallagher, looks at marriage as a marker for social and economic well-being. Gallagher points out that when marriage rates are low in a community, it is the children who suffer the most. Her major point here is that marriage is in large part an economic partnership in which two people pool their resources, support one another's lives and careers, draw upon one another's social and family networks, compensate for one another's weaknesses, share tasks in an efficient way, and work cooperatively toward the goal of financial success. Moreover, she points out that marriage itself changes behavior in ways that tend to make people financially better off.

In chapter 5, Obie Clayton and Joan Moore examine the effects of the incarceration of great numbers of black men on family formation. Currently, about a third of the African American male population is under the control of the correctional system. The authors state that efforts must be directed at preventing prison, ex-offenders, and illicit cultural icons from gaining cultural hegemony if the black family is to thrive in the future.

Part III (chapters 6 through 9) deals with contemporary issues of fatherhood within the black community. The trend of black family fragmentation that countless analysts had assumed to be all but unstoppable—signaled by yearly increases in unwed childbearing and divorce and resulting in ever greater proportions of African American children living apart from their fathers—galvanized one state, South Carolina, to take action. In chapter 6, Barbara Morrison-Rodriguez explains in detail how South Carolina dealt with the issue of father absence by bringing together representatives of the academic and faith-based communities and of the government to come up with a holistic approach to solving this problem.

In chapter 7, Wornie Reed shows how the public health intervention and prevention framework can be used to address the causes of fatherlessness. Reed points out that there is no one explanation for the decline in marriage rates but, rather, that one must look at the problem from different perspectives and identify the risk factors present at the local level.

Chapters 8 and 9 should be read together. Wade Horn (chapter 8) points out lessons learned from fatherhood programs and concludes that many programs do succeed in promoting positive fatherhood. He points out that fathers matter and that successful programs are those that intervene early in a male's life to teach responsibility. However, he also warns against perceiving any one model as a cure-all.

Enola Aird, in chapter 9, discusses the importance of marriage. From 1995 to 2000 the proportion of African American children living in two-parent, married-couple homes rose from 34.8 to 38.9 percent (Dupree and Primus 2001). Though the number remains distressingly low, more important is that it represents a significant increase in just five years and the clear cessation and even reversal of the long-term shift toward black family fragmentation. Aird posits that continuing progress on this issue may be possible.

As you read, you will quickly realize that many of the authors have varying opinions concerning marriage but that all agree that children need their fathers. It will also be readily apparent that the question of marriage and marriageability are deeply connected to the quality of the relationship between adult males and females. None of the authors in this volume discounts the suffering of many mothers and children who have lived through abusive marriages and relationships, but their focus here is on the males. Any strategy to promote black fatherhood must also stress the bonds between male and female as well as between parent and child.

## REFERENCES

Dupree, Allen, and Wendell Primus. 2001. *Declining Share of Children Lived with Single Mothers in the Late 1990s.* Washington, D.C.: Center on Budget and Policy Priorities.

Franklin, Donna L. 1997. *Ensuring Inequality: The Structural Transformation of the African-American Family.* New York: Oxford University Press.

Morehouse Research Institute and Institute for American Values. 1999. *Turning the Corner on Father Absence in Black America: A Statement from the Morehouse Conference on African American Fathers.* Atlanta: Morehouse Research Institute and Institute for American Values.

Raspberry, William. 1998. Keynote speech at "African American Fathers and their Families" convention, Atlanta, Georgia (November 5).

# PART I

## Declines in Marriage Within African American Families

# Chapter 1

## THE WOES OF THE INNER-CITY AFRICAN AMERICAN FATHER

### WILLIAM JULIUS WILSON

Today, one quarter of all families and six of every ten black families are lone-parent families, and most of these lone parents are
never-married mothers. One half of all marriages end in divorce and
only one half of divorced fathers make the payments that they owe
by law to support their children. If current trends continue, one half
of the children in the United States will experience at least part of
their childhoods in lone-parent families (Luker 1998).

The decline of the married-parent family is a controversial topic,
one that has been featured in political debates about "family values."
According to one observer,

> Ever since the growth of the one-parent family, there has been a ten-
> dency to accept it as virtually normal. Too many social commentators
> portray the birth of children out of wedlock as part of the "norm."
> What actually amounts to abandoning children, usually by the father,
> is becoming increasingly acceptable without penalty to anyone except
> to the neglected child. Too many social scientists and policymakers
> play down the advantages of the two-parent family; some even ridicule
> it as an outmoded middle-class ideal. (Hechinger 1992)

One reason for concern about the sharp decline in the marriage
rate is that children living in one-parent families in the United
States, especially those in families where the parent has never married, suffer from many more disadvantages than those in married-
parent families. "Families with multiple earners rise toward the top
of the family income distribution, while families with just one earner
fall toward the bottom," states the University of Texas economist
James K. Galbraith (1998, 12). "As the number of single-headed
households rises, so too will inequality. This pattern is compounded

in the real world by the grim fact that single-headed households also comprise, to a large extent, those with the most unstable employment experiences at the lowest wages."

Children living in households headed by single mothers are the poorest demographic group in the nation. Whereas only one tenth of children in husband-wife families are living below the poverty line, over one third of those living with divorced mothers and two thirds living with mothers who had never married are classified as poor. Finally, mothers who had never been married are more likely to receive welfare or public assistance for a significantly longer period than do separated or divorced mothers.

In addition to the strong links between single parenthood and poverty and welfare receipt, the available research indicates that children from mother-only households are more likely to be school dropouts, to receive lower earnings in young adulthood, and to be recipients of welfare. Moreover, daughters who have grown up in black single-parent households are more likely to establish single-parent households themselves than are those who have been raised in married-couple households. Furthermore, single-parent households tend to exert less control over the behavior of adolescents. Reviewing their research findings, Sanford Dornbusch and his colleagues (1985, 340) concluded:

> We do not know whether it is lack of surveillance, lack of appropriate teaching, or lack of social support for the single parent that leads to a reduction in control of adolescents, especially males, in mother-only families. But we do know, and perhaps this has broad implications, that the presence of any other adult in a mother-only household brings control levels closer to those found in two-parent families . . . and that the raising of adolescents is not a task that can be borne by a mother alone.

Many factors are involved in the precipitous decline in marriage rates and the sharp rise in lone-parent families since the 1970s. The explanation most often heard in the public debate associates the increase in the number of out-of-wedlock births and single-parent families with welfare. Indeed, it is widely assumed among the general public that a direct causal connection exists between the level of welfare benefits and the likelihood that a young woman will bear a child outside marriage, and this assumption is reflected in the many recent proposals for welfare reform.

However, the scientific evidence offers little support for the claim that AFDC benefits played a significant role in promoting out-of-wedlock births. Research examining the association between the generosity of welfare benefits and out-of-wedlock childbearing and teen pregnancy indicates that benefit levels have no significant effect on the likelihood that African American girls and women will have children outside marriage; likewise, welfare rates have either no significant effect or only a small effect on the odds that whites will have children outside marriage. There is no evidence to suggest that welfare is a major factor in the rise of childbearing outside marriage (see, for example, Duncan 1994; Duncan and Hoffman 1990; and Bane and Ellwood 1983).

The rate of out-of-wedlock teen childbearing nearly doubled between 1975 and 1995, despite the fact that during the period the real value of AFDC, food stamps, and Medicaid fell, if one adjusts for inflation. Furthermore, the smallest increases in the number of out-of-wedlock births did not occur in the states that had the largest declines in the inflation-adjusted value of AFDC benefits (Duncan 1994). Indeed, while the real value of cash welfare benefits plummeted between 1975 and 1995, not only did out-of-wedlock childbearing increase, but also postpartum marriages (marriages following the birth of a couple's child) decreased.

## FATHERHOOD IN THE INNER-CITY GHETTO

In my book *The Truly Disadvantaged* (1987), I argued that the sharp increase in black male joblessness since 1970 accounts in large measure for the rise in the rate of single-parent African American families, and that since jobless rates are highest in the inner-city ghetto, rates of single parenthood are also highest there. Still, the evidence from recent research on the relationship between employment on the one hand and rates of marriage and single parenthood on the other is mixed. Some studies reveal that a man's employment status is not related to the likelihood of his conceiving a child out of wedlock.[1]

If, however, the focus of research shifts from the birth of a child out of wedlock to the probability of the parents' subsequent entry into marriage, the employment status of the male becomes an important factor. The data that we collected in Chicago's inner-city neighborhoods in the late 1980s revealed that although the employment status of the man is unrelated to the risk of conceiving a child out of wedlock, for the younger black father employment status is strongly associated with his entry into marriage after the birth of his child. More specifically, although employment had no significant effect on the likelihood that inner-city single fathers ages thirty-two to forty-four would eventually marry, it did increase the likelihood of marriage to the mother of their children by eight times for single fathers eighteen to thirty-one (Testa 1991; Testa and Krogh 1995).

Still, although there may be a strong association between rates of marriage and employment status and earnings at any given point in time in the inner city, national longitudinal studies suggest that these factors account for only a fraction of the overall *decline* in marriage among African Americans. Joblessness matters, but there are other factors that have to be taken into account, even in the inner city.

To be more specific, in the inner-city ghetto, the norms in support of husband-wife families and against out-of-wedlock births have not only become weaker as a result of general trends in society but have also gradually disintegrated because of the sharp rise in joblessness and declining real incomes of residents of the inner city over the past several decades, especially from the mid-1970s to 1995. The weakening of social sanctions has had the greatest impact on the jobless, but it has also affected many who are employed, especially those whose jobs are not very secure or stable or those who are experiencing declining real incomes. The declining marriage rates among inner-city black parents is a function not simply of increased economic marginality or of changing attitudes toward sex and marriage but also of the interaction between the two. As Mark Testa (1991, 16), a former member of my research team in Chicago, pointed out, "[V]ariation in the moral evaluations that different . . . groups attach to premarital sex, out-of-wedlock pregnancy, and nonmarital parenthood affects the importance of economic considerations in a person's decision to marry." The weaker the norms against premarital sex, out-of-wedlock pregnancy, and nonmarital parenthood, the more economic considerations affect decisions to marry.

Some of the differences between inner-city black, white, and Hispanic nonmarital parenthood can be accounted for by the higher levels of joblessness and concentrated poverty in the black community. But even when ethnic-group variations in work activity, poverty concentration, education, and family structure are taken into account, significant differences between inner-city blacks and the other groups, especially the Mexicans, still remain (Testa 1991; Testa and Krogh

1995; Van Haitsma 1992). Accordingly, it is reasonable to consider the inclusion of culture among the interrelated factors that account for these differences.

A brief comparison of inner-city blacks and inner-city Mexicans (many of whom are immigrants) in terms of family perspectives provides some evidence for these cultural differences. Richard Taub (1991, 6), another member of our Chicago research team, points out that marriage and family ties are subjects of "frequent and intense discourse" among Mexican immigrants. Mexicans come to the United States with a clear conception of a traditional family unit that features men as breadwinners. Although extramarital affairs by men are tolerated, "a pregnant, unmarried woman is a source of opprobrium, anguish, or great concern." Pressure is applied by the kin of both parents to enter into marriage.

The family norms and behavior in inner-city black neighborhoods stand in sharp contrast. The husband-wife relationship is only weakly supported. The ethnographic data from our Chicago study reveal that the relationships between inner-city black men and women, whether in a marital or nonmarital situation, are often fractious and antagonistic. Inner-city black women routinely say that they distrust men and feel strongly that black men lack dedication to their families. They argue that black males are hopeless as either husbands or fathers and that more of their time is spent on the streets than at home.

As one woman, an unmarried welfare mother of three children from a very poor neighborhood on the South Side of Chicago, put it: "And most of the men don't have jobs. . . . The way it is, if they can get jobs then they go and get drunk or whatever." When asked if that is why she did not get married, she stated:

> I don't think I want to get married but then . . . see, you're supposed to stick to that one and that's a fantasy. You know, stick with one for the rest of your life. I've never met many people like that, have you? . . . If [women are] married and have kids, them kids come in and it seems like the men get jealous 'cause you're spending your time on them. Okay, they can get up and go anytime. A woman has to stick there all the time 'cause she got them kids behind their backs.

The women in the inner city tend to believe that black men get involved with women mainly to obtain sex or money, and that once these goals are achieved women are usually discarded. For example, one woman from a poor neighborhood on the West Side of Chicago was asked if she still saw the father of her child. She stated: "He left before the baby was born, I was about two weeks pregnant and he said that he didn't want to be bothered and I said, 'Fine—you go your way and I go mine.' "

There is a widespread feeling among women in the inner city that black males have relationships with more than one female at a time. And since some young men leave their girlfriends as soon as the women become pregnant, it is not uncommon to find a black male who has fathered at least three children by three separate women. Despite the problematic state of these relationships, sex among inner-city black teenagers is widely practiced. In the ethnographic phase of our Chicago research, the respondents reported that sex is an integral and expected aspect of the male-female relationship. Males especially feel peer pressure to be sexually active. They said that the members of their peer networks brag about their sexual encounters and that they feel obligated to reveal their own sexual exploits. Little consideration is given to the implications or consequences of sexual matters for longer-term relationships.

Whereas women blame men for the poor gender relations, men maintain that it is the women who are troublesome. The men complain that it is not easy to deal with the women's suspicions about their behavior and intentions. They also feel that women are especially attracted by material resources and that it is therefore difficult to find women who are supportive of partners with a low income.

These antagonistic relationships influence the views of both men and women about marriage. The ethnographic data reveal especially weak support for the institution of marriage among black men in the inner-city ghetto. For many of the men, marriage ties a man down and results in a loss of freedom. "Marriage. You can't have it, you can't do the things you wanna do then," stated an unemployed twenty-one-year-old unmarried father of one child from a poor neighborhood on the West Side. "She [the spouse] might want you in at a certain time and all, all this. You can't hang out when you married, you know. You married to be with her. . . . I like, you know, spending my time, half the time with my friends and then come in when I want to. . . . In my book it [marriage] is something that is bad. Like, like fighting, divorce."

A twenty-seven-year-old unmarried, employed father of one child makes a similar point: Marriage "cuts down a lot of things you used to do, like, staying out late, stuff like that, hanging with the fellows all day, like, now you can do what the hell you want to do, now, when you—when you married, got a family, it cuts a lot of that stuff off."

The men in the inner city generally tend to feel that it is much better for all parties to remain in a nonmarital relationship until the relationship dissolves rather than to get married and then have to get a divorce. A twenty-five-year-old unmarried West Side resident, the father of one child, expressed this view:

Well, most black men feel now, why get married when you got six to seven womens to one guy, really. You know, 'cause there's more women out here mostly than men. 'Cause most dudes around here are killing each other like fools over drugs or all this other stuff. And if you're not that bad-looking of a guy, you know, and you know a lot of women like you, why get married when you can play the field the way they want to do, you know?

An eighteen-year-old senior in high school and father of a five-week-old son described why he was not ready for marriage at the present time.

I don't think that marriage is for me right now, but I think that there is a certain age where I think that I would want to get married to somebody that I really love. I say that I would be about twenty-five years old, but right now I don't have it on my conscience. I'm always farsighted for the future but not marriage, but like I said, at a certain age I will probably decide on doing that.

No, that is not on my conscience right now. A lot of people, they tell me don't get married because once you stay with that one woman you probably start having problems. I know a lot of boyfriends and girlfriends, you know they have problems but then when they decide to get married I don't think things will turn out right. I just feel that I have a child by her and I am going to go ahead and support that child, but thinking about marriage I ain't got it on my conscience right now.

A twenty-five-year-old man with a part-time job who had a seven-year-old daughter explained why he avoided marriage following the child's birth:

For years I have been observing other marriages. They all have been built on the wrong foundation. The husband misuses the family or neglects the family or the wife do the same, ah, they just missing a lot of important elements. I had made a commitment to marry her really out of people pleasing. My mom wanted me to do it; her parents wanted us to do it. Taking their suggestions and opinions about the situation over my own and [I] am a grown man. These decisions is for me to make and I realized that they were going to go to expect it to last for twenty, forty years, so I evaluated my feelings and came to the honest conclusion that [it] was not right for me, right. And I made the decision that the baby, that I could be a father without necessarily living there.

Others talk about avoiding or delaying marriage for economic reasons. "It made no sense to just get married because we have a baby like other people . . . do," argued an eighteen-year-old unmarried father of a two-week-old son. "If I couldn't take care of my family, why get married?"

Thus, our ethnographic data suggest that for many inner-city men, marriage is not a desirable option. The dominant attitude among the young single black fathers is, "I'll get married in the future when I am no longer having fun and when I get a job or a better job" (Laseter 1994). Marriage limits their ability to date other women or "hang out" with the boys. The ethnographic data clearly reveal that the birth of a child does not create a sense of obligation to marry, and that most young fathers feel little pressure, from either their own or their partner's family, to marry. Having children and getting married are not usually connected.

There is very little research on changing norms and sanctions regarding the family in the inner city, but there does seem to be some indication that the norms have changed. In a study of fathering in the inner city based on a series of interviews with the same respondents over several years, Frank Furstenberg (1994, 15), a University of Pennsylvania sociologist, notes:

I have no way of knowing for sure, but I think that families now exert less pressure on men to remain involved than they once did. I found no instance, for example, of families urging their children to marry or even to live together as was common when I was studying the parents of my informants in the mid-1960s.

Yet the data from our study indicate that young men do "feel some obligation to contribute something to support their children" (Laseter 1994, 40). The level of financial support is low and often erratic, however, varying from occasionally buying disposable diapers to regularly contributing several hundred dollars a month.

As Furstenberg (1994, 29) points out,

> When ill-timed pregnancies occur in unstable partnerships to men who have few material resources for managing unplanned parenthood, they challenge, to say the least, the commitment of young fathers. Fatherhood occurs to men who often have a personal biography that poorly equips them to act on their intentions, even when their intentions to do for their children are strongly felt. And fatherhood [in the inner city] takes place in a culture where the gap between good intentions and good performance is large and widely recognized.

Black women in the inner city are more interested in marriage, but their expectations for matrimony are low and they do not hold the men they encounter in very high regard. The women feel that even if they do marry, it is unlikely to be successful. They maintain that husbands are not as dedicated to their wives as in previous generations and that they would not be able to depend on their husbands even if they did get married.

A young welfare mother of three children from a poor neighborhood on the West Side of Chicago made the following point:

> Well, to my recollection, twenty years ago I was only seven years [old] but . . . twenty years ago, men, if they got a woman pregnant, that if they didn't marry her, they stood by her and took care of the child. And nowadays, when a man makes you pregnant, they're goin' off and leave you and think nothing of it. And also . . . also, uh, twenty years ago, I find that there were more people getting married and when they got married they were staying together. I found that with a lot of couples nowadays, that when they get married they're so quick to get a divorce. I've thought about marriage myself many times, uh, but nowadays, it seems to me that when it comes to marriage, it just doesn't mean anything to people. At least the men that I talk to. And also, twenty years ago, I think families were closer. I found now families are drifting apart, they're not as loving as they were twenty years ago. I find with a lot of families now, they're quicker to hurt you than to help you.

Finally, a twenty-seven-year-old single woman—she is childless, has four years of college, works as a customer-service representative, and lives in a poor neighborhood on the South Side—talked about changes in family structure in relation to her own personal situation. According to her, there has been

> a definite change in the family structure as far as the mother and father being together. The way things are going now you'll find more single women having kids, but not totally dependent on the guy being there. I know there's a change in friends of mine who have kids, the father isn't there with them. They're not so totally dependent on him any more. They're out there doing for themselves. . . . You have to make it one way or another, and you can't depend on him to come through or him to be there.

The ethnographic data reveal that both inner-city black males and females believe that since most marriages will eventually break up and since marriages no longer represent meaningful relationships, it is better to avoid the entanglements of wedlock altogether. For many single mothers in the inner city, nonmarriage makes more sense as a family-formation strategy than does marriage. Single mothers who perceive the fathers of their children as unreliable or as having limited financial means will often—rationally—choose single parenthood. From the point of view of day-to-day survival, single parenthood reduces the emotional burden and shields them from the type of exploitation that often accompanies the sharing of both living arrangements and limited resources. Men and women are extremely suspicious of each other, and their concerns range from the degree of financial commitment to fidelity. For all these reasons, they often state they do not want to get married until they are sure it is going to work out.

Changing patterns of family formation are not limited to the inner-city black community; they are part of a current societal trend. The commitment to traditional husband-wife families and the stigma associated with separation, divorce, and out-of-wedlock births have weakened significantly in the United States. "The labor market conditions which sustained the 'male breadwinner' family have all but vanished" (Breslau 1991, 11). This has gradually led to the creation of a new set of orientations that places less value on marriage and rejects the actual dominance of men as a standard for a successful husband-wife family (Taub 1991).

The major argument I have advanced is this: inner-city black single parents, unlike their Mexican-immigrant counterparts, feel little pressure to commit to a marriage. They emphasize the loss of free-dom, the lack of dedication to one's partner, and the importance of having secure jobs and financial security before seriously consider-ing matrimony. They have little reason to contemplate seriously the consequences of single parenthood because their prospects for social and economic mobility are severely limited whether they are married or not.

These responses represent a linkage between new structural reali-ties, changing norms, and evolving cultural patterns. The new struc-tural realities may be seen in the diminishing employment opportu-nities for low-skilled workers. As employment prospects recede, the foundation for stable relationships becomes weaker over time. More permanent relationships such as marriage give way to temporary liaisons that result in broken relationships, out-of-wedlock pregnan-cies and births, and, to a lesser extent, separation and divorce. The changing norms concerning marriage in the larger society reinforce the movement toward temporary liaisons in the inner city, and there-fore economic considerations in marital decisions take on even greater weight. The evolving cultural patterns may be seen in the sharing of negative outlooks toward marriage and toward the relationships between males and females in the inner city, outlooks that are devel-oped in and influenced by an environment plagued by persistent job-lessness. This combination of factors has increased out-of-wedlock births, weakened the family structure, and expanded the welfare rolls.

The intensity of the commitment to the marital bond among Mex-ican immigrants will very likely decline the longer they remain in the United States and are exposed to U.S. norms, patterns of behavior, and changing opportunity structures for men and women. Nonethe-less, cultural arrangements reflect structural realities. In comparison with African Americans in the inner city, Mexican immigrants have a more secure attachment to the labor force, as well as stronger house-holds, networks, and neighborhoods. Therefore, as long as these differences exist, attitudes toward the family and family formation among inner-city blacks and Mexican immigrants will contrast noticeably.

In communities where the young people have little reason to believe that they have a promising future—including the prospects of stable employment and stable marriages—the absence of strong normative pressure to resolve out-of-wedlock pregnancies through marriage has resulted in an explosion of single-parent families. In such communities, adolescents and young adults are more likely to engage in behavior that jeopardizes their chances for social and economic mobility. For example, the teenagers most likely to bear a child are those with the least to lose. "Young people who are raised with a sense of opportunity and are able realistically to picture a better life are often successful in avoiding the draw of the street culture," notes Elijah Anderson (1991). But far too few girls in the inner-city ghetto can realize such dreams. For them, having a baby proves that they are attractive to "desirable (good-looking) men. Such recognition from peers, along with the status of grown woman, which accrues to her upon becoming a mother, is often the most she hopes for."

A thirty-year-old welfare mother of two children from an impoverished South Side neighborhood of Chicago put it this way: "A lot of them is having babies 'cause they ain't got nothing better to do. Now I have one thirteen and one eight years old. I had mine when I was sixteen years old. I had mine 'cause I was curious. I wanted to see what it was like" (Anderson 1991, 397).

Over thirty years ago, the famous black psychologist Kenneth B. Clark pinpointed this problem in distinguishing the way that poor black ghetto residents and those of the black middle class approach the issue of sex. Clark pointed out (1965, 71–72) that the attitude toward sex among black middle-class families is vastly different from that among the ghetto poor. For the middle-class African American girl, as for her middle-class white counterpart, sex is tied to aspirations and status. "She wants to make a good marriage . . . and the motivation to avoid illegitimate pregnancy is great." On the other hand, the young people in the inner-city ghetto, involved in tentative and sporadic relationships, pursue acceptance, love, and affection more desperately than young people in other neighborhoods. For many, person-to-person relationships compensate for society's rejection. The boy and girl in the inner-city ghetto are "forced to be quite elemental in their demands, and sex becomes more important for them than even they realize," stated Clark. "They act in a cavalier fashion about their affairs, trying to seem casual and cool, but it is clear nonetheless that they are dominated by the complexity of their needs."

Neither the girl nor the boy in the ghetto has any illusions. Realistic about the nature of her situation, the girl does not expect to hold on to the boy. "Sex is important to her but it is not, as in middle-class society, a symbol of status, to be used to rise into a better family class or a higher income bracket" (Clark 1965, 72). Rather, sex is used to gain personal affirmation. "She is desired and that is almost enough." If the relationship results in an out-of-wedlock birth, the child's acceptance is unambiguous. An illegitimate child in the ghetto is not stigmatized. There is no ultimate disgrace, no demand for abortion, no pressure to give up the child to an adoption agency such as one finds in more advantaged neighborhoods. The stigma of illegitimacy in the middle class derives from personal and family aspirations. The girl from a poor inner-city ghetto family, however, only sacrifices a few of her already limited options by having a child out of wedlock.

As Clark (1965, 73) put it, "She is not going to make a 'better marriage' or improve her economic and social status either way. On the contrary, a child is a symbol of the fact that she is a woman, and she may gain from having something on her own." Likewise, the boy who fathers a child out of wedlock has little to lose because his prospects for social and economic mobility are bleak or nonexistent. Reflecting on the prevalence of births outside marriage in the ghetto, Clark (1965, 73) stated:

> Illegitimacy in the ghetto cannot be understood or dealt with in terms of punitive hostility, as in the suggestion that unwed mothers be denied welfare if illegitimacy is repeated. Such approaches obscure, with empty and at times hypocritical moralizing, the desperate yearning of the young for acceptance and identity, the need to be meaningful to someone else even for a moment without implication of a pledge of foreverness. If, when the girl becomes pregnant, the boy deserts or refuses to marry her, it is often because neither can sustain an intimate relationship; both seem incapable of the tenderness that continues beyond immediate gratification. Both may have a realistic, if unconscious, acceptance of the fact that nothing else is possible; to expect— to ask—for more would be to open oneself to the inevitable rejections, hurts, and frustrations.

## ADDRESSING THE PROBLEMS OF INNER-CITY FATHERHOOD

It is often assumed that welfare reform will lead to a reduction of out-of-wedlock births in poor urban neighborhoods and will force fathers to assume greater responsibility for the care of their children. The Personal Responsibility and Work Opportunity Reconciliation Act of 1996, otherwise known as the welfare reform act, includes strong provisions to establish the paternity of out-of-wedlock children in order to enhance child-support payments by these men. Many states impose penalties on welfare recipients who refuse to identify the absent father—the most extreme penalty being the total loss of welfare benefits. But unless the employment opportunities in inner-city ghetto neighborhoods are enhanced for absent fathers, it is unrealistic to assume that they will be able to consistently fulfill their child-support obligations. This is especially true of low-income inner-city black males, who face two serious problems: the decreased relative demand for low-skilled labor, and negative employer attitudes. Let me focus briefly on these two problems.

Blacks still confront racial barriers in the labor market, but this is not the only source of their problems. Many of the problems of low-skilled inner-city African American workers stem from changes in the demand for labor in the global economy, which are related to three factors. The first is the computer revolution, the spread of new technologies that have displaced low-skilled workers and rewarded the more highly trained. The second is the rapid growth in college enrollment, which has increased the supply and reduced the cost of skilled labor. The third factor is the growing internationalization of economic activity, including trade liberalization policies that have increased the competition of low-skilled workers in this country with low-skilled workers around the world. In general, highly educated or highly skilled workers have benefited from all these changes, whereas lower-skilled workers face the growing threat of job displacement and eroding wages (Katz 1996; Schwartzman 1997).

One of the consequences of historic racism in America is that a disproportionate number of African Americans are unskilled. Accordingly, the decreased relative demand for low-skilled labor has had a greater impact on blacks than on whites. Although the number of skilled blacks (including managers, professionals, and technicians) has increased sharply in the last several years, the proportion of those who are unskilled remains large, because the black population, burdened by cumulative experiences of racial restrictions, was overwhelmingly unskilled just several decades ago. Since the proportion of African American workers who are low-skilled is relatively large, the impact of the decreased relative demand for low-skilled labor is strongly felt in the black community (Schwartzman 1997).

Nonetheless, there is a tendency among policymakers, scholars, and black leaders alike to separate the economic problems in the inner-city black community from national and international trends affecting American families and neighborhoods. If the economic problems of the inner city are defined solely in racial terms they can be isolated and viewed as only requiring race-based solutions as proposed by those on the left, or narrow political solutions with subtle racial connotations, such as welfare reform, as strongly advocated by those on the right.

New research into urban labor markets by the economist Harry Holzer (1996) of Michigan State University reveals the magnitude of the problem. Surveying 3,000 employers in Atlanta, Boston, Detroit, and Los Angeles, Holzer found that workers today need to have the basic skills of reading, writing, and performing arithmetic calculations even for the most entry-level jobs. Most employers require a high school degree, particular kinds of previous work experience, and job references. Because of the large oversupply of low-skilled workers relative to the number of low-skilled jobs, many poorly educated and poorly trained individuals have difficulty finding jobs even when the local labor market is strong (Holzer 1996; Center on Budget and Policy Priorities 1996).

The problem is that in recent years, except for the period of prolonged low unemployment in the latter 1990s and 2000, tight labor markets, which are advantageous for workers, have been of relatively short duration and frequently have been followed by a recession that either wiped out previous gains for many workers or did not allow others to fully recover from a previous period of economic stagnation. It would take sustained tight labor markets over many years to draw back discouraged inner-city workers who have dropped out of the labor market altogether, some for very long periods of time.

The United States has recently ended one of the longest economic recoveries in the last half century. The signs for disadvantaged groups in this economy were encouraging as the ranks of those out of work for more than six months declined from almost 2 million in January 1993 to about 700,000 in December 2000. Moreover, the unemployment rate for high school dropouts declined by 6 percentage poir' from 12 percent in 1992 to just 6 percent at the end of 2000, and of this decline occurred since 1997. Furthermore, the black ur ment rate dipped to 7 percent in November 2000, the low' Bureau of Labor Statistics began collecting data by rac

If the recent economic boom had lasted for sevr would have been the best antidote for low-skillᵼ employment and earning prospects had diminished in the late twentieth century. For example, in America's inner cities the extension of the economic recovery for several more years would have significantly lowered the over all jobless rate not only for the low-skilled workers who are still in the labor force but also for those who have been outside the labor market for many years.

But given the decreased relative demand for low-skilled labor, what will happen to these workers as the economy slows down? Considering the changing nature of the economy, there is little reason to think that their prospects will be anything but bleak. Although the relative importance of the different underlying causes contributing to the growing job problems of the less-skilled, including those in the inner city, continue to be debated, there is little disagreement among economists about the underlying trends themselves, and these are unlikely to reverse themselves. In short, over a sustained period the labor market in the United States has twisted against disadvantaged workers—those with limited skills or education who come from poor families and neighborhoods—and this has greatly diminished their actual and potential earnings (Katz 1996).

For inner-city black workers, the problems created by the decreased relative demand for labor are exacerbated by negative employer attitudes. As one inner-city manufacturer from our study put it, when discussing where employers look for new workers, "When we hear other employers talk, they'll go after primarily the Hispanic and Oriental first, those two, and, I'll qualify that even further, the Mexican Hispanic, and any Oriental, and after that, that's pretty much it, that's pretty much where they like to draw the line, right there" (Wilson 1996).

Interviews of a representative sample of Chicago-area employers by our research team show that a substantial majority considered inner-city black males to be uneducated, unstable, uncooperative, or dishonest. For example, a suburban drug store manager said, "It's unfortunate, but in my business I think overall [black men] tend to be known to be dishonest. I think that's too bad but that's the image they have."

INTERVIEWER: "So you think it's an image problem?"
RESPONDENT: "Yeah, a dishonest, an image problem of being dishonest men and lazy. They're known to be lazy. They are. [*Laughs*] I hate to tell you, but. It's all an image, though. Whether they are or not, I don't know, but, it's an image that is perceived."

INTERVIEWER: "I see. How do you think that image was developed?"
RESPONDENT: "Go look in the jails." [*Laughs*]

Concerns about theft prompted the owner of a suburban electrical services firm to offer this unique explanation as to why he would not hire inner-city black ghetto males:

If you're in a white neighborhood . . . and you have a manufacturing firm and a ghetto person comes there to apply, it doesn't make any difference what color his skin is. . . . If you know that's where he's from you know several things. One is that if you give him a job there, he's going to be unbelievably pressured to give information to his peer group in the ghetto . . . about the security system, the comings and goings of what's of value there that we could rip off. He's not a crook. He wants no part of it. But he lives in an area where he may be physically or in danger of his life if he doesn't provide the information to the people that live around him. As a manager, I know that. And I'm not going to hire him because of that. I'm not discriminating against him because he's black, I'm discriminating against him because he has a problem that he's going to bring to me. Now the fact that he is black and it happens that the people around him are black is only coincidental. In Warsaw they were Jews. They had the same problem.

The president of an inner-city manufacturing firm in Chicago expressed a different concern about employing black males from certain inner-city neighborhoods, saying, "If somebody gave me their address, uh, Cabrini Green, I might unavoidably have some concerns."

INTERVIEWER: What would your concerns be?
RESPONDENT: That the poor guy probably would be frequently unable to get to work and . . . I probably would watch him more carefully even if it wasn't fair, than I would with somebody else. I know what I should do, though, is recognize that here's a guy that is trying to get out of his situation and probably will work harder than somebody else who's already out of there and he might be the best one around here. But I, I think I would have to struggle accepting that premise at the beginning.

Given such attitudes, the lack of black access to the informal job networks is a particular problem for black males, as revealed in the following comments by an employer:

All of a sudden, they take a look at a guy, and unless he's got an in, the reason why I hired this black kid the last time is cause my neighbor said to me, yeah I used him for a few [days], he's good, and I said, you know what, I'm going to take a chance. But it was a recommendation. But other than that, I've got a walk-in, and, who knows? And I think that for the most part, a guy sees a black man, he's a bit hesitant, because, I don't know.

The restructuring of the economy will continue to compound the negative effects of the perceptions of inner-city black males. Because of the increasing shift to service industries, employers have a greater need for workers who can effectively serve and relate to the consumer. Black males are not perceived to have such qualities.

Thus, the attitudes that many inner-city black males express about their jobs and job prospects reflect their plummeting position in a changing labor market. The more they complain and manifest their dissatisfaction, the less desirable they seem to employers. They therefore experience greater discrimination when they seek employment and clash more often with supervisors when they find employment. It is therefore important to link attitudinal and other cultural traits with structural realities.

For all these reasons, programs to address the problems of fatherhood in poor inner-city communities are bound to fail if they ignore the interaction of cultural traits and structural realities. As Jal Mehta (1999) of Harvard University has correctly pointed out, conservatives make a fundamental mistake when they assume that the behaviors of individuals can "somehow be separated from the circumstances in which they live." I have argued elsewhere that socially isolated ghetto neighborhoods, plagued by high rates of joblessness, will have low collective efficacy in terms of reaching mainstream goals, which in turn decreases individual self-efficacy. In the more socially isolated ghetto neighborhoods, networks of kin, friends, and associates are more likely to include a higher proportion of individuals who, because of their experiences with extreme economic marginality, tend to doubt that they can achieve approved societal goals. The self-doubts may exist for either of two reasons: these individuals may have questions concerning their own capabilities or preparedness, or they may perceive that severe restrictions have been imposed on them by a hostile environment (Wilson 1996).

The longer the joblessness persists, the more likely it is that these self-doubts will take root. I think it is reasonable to assume that the association between joblessness and self-efficacy grows over time and becomes stronger the longer a neighborhood is plagued by low employment. This hypothesis cannot be directly tested, but my assumption is that there are lower levels of self-efficacy in the inner city today with respect to people's ability to satisfy mainstream goals than there were in previous years, when most of the adults were working and were involved in informal job networks.

An individual's feelings of low self-efficacy grow out of experiences involving unstable work and low income and are reinforced or strengthened by the similar feelings and views of others who share the conditions and culture of the neighborhood. This represents what anthropologists call accidental cultural transmission, whereby the individual's exposure to certain attitudes and actions is so frequent that they actually become part of his or her own perspective. In the inner-city ghetto, the end result of this dynamic is lower collective efficacy. Research on the *transmission* of such views and feelings would represent a cultural analysis of life in poverty. The psychological self-efficacy theory is used here not in isolation but in relation to the *structural problem* of weak labor-force attachment (unstable work, joblessness, and low income) because of restricted opportunities and the *cultural problem* of the transmission of self and collective beliefs in the neighborhood.

As I see it, the decreased commitment to fatherhood in the inner city is a cultural problem that grows out of restricted opportunities and constraints. Whether they are willing to admit it or not, many inner-city fathers have low self-efficacy when it comes to fatherhood. The norms of fatherhood include an obligation to provide adequate and consistent material support for your spouse and children. Enduring lack of success in the labor market, for all the reasons cited, decreases the ability of many inner-city men to provide adequately for their children, which in turn lowers their self-confidence as providers and creates antagonistic relations with their child's mother. This often results in convenient rationalizations—shared and reinforced by other men in similar situations—that reject the institution of marriage in ways that enhance, not diminish, their self-esteem. The end result is a failure to meet the societal norms of fatherhood.

Accordingly, programs that focus on the cultural problems pertaining to fatherhood without addressing adequately the broader and more fundamental issue of structural constraints or limited opportunities are likely to fail or have limited success. In my view, the most effective programs to enhance fatherhood in the inner city will be those that address behaviors, attitudes, and norms, while at the same time focusing on ways to open the structure of opportunity so that fathers can realistically envision a better life for themselves and get a real chance to care adequately for their children.

---

This chapter includes paragraphs, some rewritten, from my book, *When Work Disappears: The World of the New Urban Poor* (New York: Knopf, 1996).

## NOTES

1. See Testa (1991) for a review of these studies.

## REFERENCES

Anderson, Elijah. 1991. "Neighborhood Effects on Teenage Pregnancy." In *The Urban Underclass*, edited by Christopher Jencks and Paul E. Peterson. Washington, D.C.: Brookings Institution Press.

Bane, Mary Jo, and David Ellwood. 1983. "Slipping into and out of Poverty: The Dynamics of Spells." Working paper no. 1199. Cambridge, Mass.: National Bureau of Economic Research.

Breslau, Daniel. 1991. "Reciprocity and Gender in Low-Income Households." Paper presented at the Chicago Urban Poverty and Family Life Conference, Chicago, Illinois. (October 10–12).

Center on Budget and Policy Priorities. 1996. *The Administration's $3 Billion Jobs Proposal*. Washington, D.C.: Center on Budget and Policy Priorities.

Clark, Kenneth B. 1965. *Dark Ghetto: Dilemmas of Social Power*. New York: Harper & Row.

Dornbusch, Sanford M., J. Merrill Carlsmith, Steven J. Bushwall, Philip L. Ritter, Herbert Leiderman, Albert H. Hastorf, and Ruth T. Gross. 1985. "Single Parents, Extended Households, and the Control of Adolescents." *Child Development* 56(April): 326–41.

Duncan, Greg J. 1994. Testimony before the Subcommittee on Human Resources of the Committee on Ways and Means Hearing on Early Childbearing. Washington, D.C. (July 29).

Duncan, Greg J., and Saul D. Hoffman. 1990. "Welfare Benefits, Economic Opportunities, and Out-of-Wedlock Births Among Black Teenage Girls." *Demography* 27(November 4): 519–35.

Furstenberg, Frank F. 1994. "Fathering in the Inner City: Paternal Participation and Public Policy." Unpublished manuscript, University of Pennsylvania.

Galbraith, James K. 1998. *Created Unequal: The Crisis in American Pay*. New York: Free Press.

Hechinger, Fred M. 1992. *Fateful Choices*. New York: Hill & Wang.

Holzer, Harry. 1996. *What Employers Want: Job Prospects for Less Educated Workers*. New York: Russell Sage Foundation.

Katz, Lawrence. 1996. "Wage Subsidies for the Disadvantaged." Working paper 5679. Cambridge, Mass.: National Bureau of Economic Research.

Laseter, R. 1994. "Young Inner-City African American Men: Work and Family Life." Ph.D. diss., University of Chicago.

Luker, Kristin. 1998. *Dubious Conceptions: The Politics of Teenage Pregnancy*. Cambridge, Mass.: Harvard University Press.

Metha, Jal David. 1999. "Efficacy and the New Social Stratification: Explaining Why the Black Poor Stay Poor in a Post-discriminatory Era." B.A. honors thesis. Cambridge: Harvard University.

Schwartzman, David. 1997. *Black Unemployment: Part of Unskilled Unemployment*. Westport, Conn.: Greenwood Press.

Taub, Richard. 1991. "Differing Conceptions of Honor and Orientations Toward Work and Marriage Among Low-Income African-Americans and Mexican-Americans." Paper presented at the Chicago Urban Poverty and Family Life Conference, Chicago, Illinois (October 10–12).

Testa, Mark. 1991. "Male Joblessness, Nonmarital Parenthood and Marriage." Paper presented at the Chicago Urban Poverty and Family Life Conference, Chicago, Illinois (October 10–12).

Testa, Mark, and Marilyn Krogh. 1995. "The Effect of Employment on Marriage Among Black Males in Inner-City Chicago." In *The Decline in Marriage Among African Americans: Causes, Consequences and Policy Implications*, edited by M. Belinda Tucker and Claudia Mitchell-Kernan. New York: Russell Sage Foundation.

Van Haitsma, Martha. 1992. "The Social Context of Nonemployment: Blacks and Immigrant Mexicans in Chicago's Poverty Areas." Paper presented at the annual meeting of the Social Science History Association, Chicago, Illinois (November 5–8).

Wilson, William Julius. 1987. *The Truly Disadvantaged: The Inner City, the Underclass, and Public Policy*. Chicago: University of Chicago Press.

———. 1996. *When Work Disappears: The World of the New Urban Poor*. New York: Alfred A. Knopf.

# Chapter 2

## Marriage and Fatherhood in the Lives of African American Men

### Steven L. Nock

Marriage and fatherhood are important aspects of most men's lives, and they typically lead to predictable changes, especially when the two occur together. For example, research on fatherhood outside of marriage found that it has many of the same consequences for men five to ten years later in their lives that motherhood outside of marriage has for women. Men who become fathers outside of marriage go on to have lower incomes, less education, work fewer weeks per year, and have higher rates of poverty (Lerman and Ooms 1993; Moore 1995; Nock 1998a). Since unmarried men do not typically live with their children, why would premarital fatherhood have such consequences?

The simplest answer appears to be that unmarried fathers have much lower marriage rates than comparable men who are not fathers (unmarried mothers, likewise, have lower marriage rates than women who do not bear children outside of marriage). That is, once they become fathers they are less likely to marry than are comparable men who do not become fathers. The implication is that a *failure to marry* might explain some of the negative consequences of unmarried fatherhood. Indeed, research shows that the major reason premarital fatherhood affects men's futures is because it makes them less likely to ever get married and more likely to cohabit instead. Men who became fathers before marriage but who subsequently married someone (the mother of their child, or someone else) resembled men who did not become fathers before marriage. In other words, marriage erased most of the negative consequences of premarital fatherhood (Nock 1998a; Waite and Lillard 1991).

Even if the failure to marry is the primary reason that unmarried fatherhood jeopardizes men's futures, we are still left to explain why marriage has such effects. *Marriage in Men's Lives* (Nock 1998b) was an attempt to identify why marriage is generally beneficial for men. Some conclusions from that work set the stage for the following discussion:

- Both sexes gain from marriage, but men are the greater beneficiaries.

- Marriage improves men's economic, emotional, and physical well-being.

- Anything that separates men from marriage is likely to limit their futures.

- The benefits of marriage are greater when children are born to the couple.

Marriage alone improves men's lives, but not as much as marriage combined with fatherhood. Fatherhood alone is likely to be costly to men unless it is preceded or at least followed by marriage. Unfortunately, men who become unwed fathers are less likely ever to marry. As a result, they are less likely to enjoy the benefits of marriage.

Marriage occupies a less conspicuous role in black men's lives today than in the past. As William Wilson (1980, 1990) and Elijah Anderson (1990) have noted, fewer black men now marry. U.S. census figures (U.S. Bureau of the Census 1978, 1988, 1998, 2000) show that in 1977, seven in ten (69 percent) black men aged 40 to 44 were married and living with their wives. Ten years later, in 1987, the figure had dropped by thirteen percentage points, to 56 percent. In 1997, the figure had dropped another thirteen percentage points, when 43 percent of black men that age were married and living with their wives (in 2000 the figure climbed slightly, to 45 percent).

Given the high rates of divorce and separation among African Americans, another perspective on the role of marriage is gained by considering the percentage of men who have ever married. Approximately one in ten black men (9 percent) is currently married but not living with his wife. Another 16 percent are divorced. In all, seven in ten (70 percent) black men between the ages of forty and forty-four have been or are currently married. Alternatively, one in three (29 percent) men this age have never married (U.S. Bureau of the Census 2000). As these figures show, marriage is the norm among African

American men this age, although high rates of divorce and separation mean that large numbers are not currently living with their wives.

## EXPLAINING THE BENEFITS OF MARRIAGE FOR MEN

There are notable differences between married and never-married men. On a range of important dimensions married black men do better than never-married black men. The 1995 March Supplement to the U.S. Census Bureau's Current Population Survey (U.S. Bureau of the Census 1999) shows that 83 percent of working age (twenty-five to sixty-four years old) married black men were employed in March 1995 as compared with 67 percent of never-married black men in that age group. Seven percent of married black men this age are below the poverty level, as compared to 19 percent of never-married black men this age. The median annual income for married black men between the ages of 25 and 64 was $27,000, compared with $14,560 for never-married black men. Differences in educational attainment are much smaller. Married and never-married black men do not differ very much with respect to higher education. About half (48 percent) of married black males aged twenty-five to sixty-four have some education beyond high school, compared with 40 percent of never-married black men in this age group (original analysis of the March 1995 CPS by the author; Sorensen 1998).

Why is marriage associated with such significant differences in income, poverty, and labor-force participation? Part of the answer is found by considering what marriage and fatherhood say about someone to other people. Is the married man treated differently than the bachelor? Do employers make assumptions about an applicant on the basis of his marital status? Do other people expect married men to act and think differently from unmarried men? People and society in general base many of their assumptions about a man on his marital status. For example, automobile insurance rates are higher for unmarried than married young men. Likewise, life insurance is more expensive for unmarried than married men. Insurance companies make assumptions about men on the basis of their marital status because it is known that married and single men have different rates of accidents, illnesses, and deaths. Ordinary people also make comparable assumptions about men on the basis of their marital status.

Moreover, most husbands themselves understand and accept the idea that married men are expected to be different than bachelors. Once married, they have different reasons to work, accept responsibility, and honor their commitments—in other words, the *incentives* have been altered. Also, to the extent that husbands accept the legitimacy of marriage and internalize ideas associated with it, they appear to want to conform to the standards of married life—in other words, their *preferences* have been altered. As husbands they are expected to be more reliable than unmarried men, and they internalize these expectations by thinking and acting like husbands.

Economists refer to this as the "signaling" function of marriage. An economic signal is something one does that alters other people's beliefs or conveys information to them (Rowthorn 2002, 135). Such economic signals tell others such as employers, creditors, and co-workers about the type of person one is. To be most effective, such signals must be relatively costly to acquire—good examples are a college degree, a specialized skill, or credit worthiness. Marriage functions as a signal because it is costly. Husbands place significant limits on their behaviors both in the present and in future by getting married. What, then, is conveyed by the signal of marriage? Simply, the core set of assumptions surrounding marriage. Among other things, a man signals that he is willing to accept long-term commitments and responsibilities, that he is mature, that he is committed to working to support his family, that he is willing to accept responsibility for any children he fathers, and, of course, that he is heterosexual. Do such signals matter? The answer is found by asking whether husbands are treated differently than other men. Are they trusted more? Given more responsibilities? Offered better jobs? The evidence already presented would seem to indicate that the answer to all these questions is yes.

In sum, the assumptions made about a man because of his marital status influence how he is treated. They also influence the way men view themselves. Behind the many beliefs about marriage are some powerful truths that have held constant for over a century. Married people are generally healthier, live longer, earn more, have better mental health, better sex lives, and are happier than their unmarried counterparts. Further, married individuals have lower rates of suicide, fatal accidents, acute and chronic illnesses, alcoholism, and depression than the unmarried (Waite 1995; Waite and Gallagher 2000).

Married men arrange much of their lives in accordance with expectations of them as husbands. The traits expected of married men as husbands are the same traits expected of husbands as *good men*—responsibility (for wife and children), maturity, and fidelity. In this sense, marriage is a metaphor for many other aspects of men's lives. As a husband, a man is expected to be an active, independent provider who can be counted on to remain faithful to his family. In fact, married men *are* more productive and achieve more than bachelors. They are less dependent on others.

Once married, men are more likely to become members of a church and less likely to spend time with friends. Once married, men drop their involvement in informal groups in favor of more formal organizations. Men are more likely to spend time with their relatives once they are married. They are also more likely to give help and money, especially to kin (Nock 1998b). The prevailing model of marriage in America views husbands as mature, faithful, generous fathers and providers. Good husbands are expected to achieve, to help others, and to remain true to their promises. *Good husbands are seen as good men.*

To determine how much marriage affects black men, a large national survey that had followed the same individuals yearly since 1979 was analyzed. The U.S. Department of Labor's National Longitudinal Survey of Youth (NLSY) is fully representative of Americans who were between 14 and 21 years old in 1979—those born between 1958 and 1965. In 1979, 1,610 black men participated in the study. By 1993, 1,355 were still members of the study. The results are based on 15 years of annual interviews, and show how the lives of these men changed as a result of births and marriages.

## PREMARITAL BIRTHS

The research begins by focusing on fatherhood before marriage. It then focuses on marriage, and concludes with marital fatherhood. About a third (38 percent) of the black men in this study fathered at least one child before marriage. Half of the men (50 percent) married at some point in the study, and a little over a third (37 percent) had children in their marriages.

The median age at first nonmarital birth is twenty-five. This is an important finding because it means that the majority of such births occur to men well before the typical age at first marriage, which was twenty-six for men in this birth cohort (U.S. Bureau of the Census 1998). The obvious question is whether such births have an effect on black men's marriage patterns. The results suggest strongly that they do.

Before presenting the results, it is necessary to consider the problem of self-selection. It is possible that the type of man who has children outside of marriage is a different type of man than the one who does not. If that were the case, comparing the two groups of men could be misleading because differences between them might not be the result of unmarried fatherhood but would be likely anyway. This is a well known problem, and there are conventional approaches for dealing with it. In this research, two such strategies were used. First, longitudinal information about the same men focuses on how these men's lives changed before and after he has a child outside of marriage or before and after he marries. Second, demographic multivariate statistical techniques were used to eliminate as many early-life (before age twenty-one) differences as possible between unmarried fathers and men who are not fathers before the groups were compared. Specific differences that were measured and eliminated as variable were those associated with health problems (any health problem sufficient to limit a young man's ability to work), alcohol use (drinking two or more drinks a week before the man was age fourteen), trouble in school (suspended, expelled), trouble with police (arrested, stopped, or convicted of any offense other than traffic), scores on the Armed Forces Qualifying Test, family background (mother's education, intact family), urban versus rural residence, and age. Each of these factors might be associated with having children outside of marriage, marrying or remaining single, or many of the other factors investigated. Even though there may be other factors that distinguish the two types of men, the combination of multivariate controls and the use of longitudinal panel data (the same men followed year after year) provides minimal assurances that most such confounding factors have been eliminated.

## MARRIAGE AND COHABITATION

After eliminating all the factors just mentioned, black men who have children outside of marriage have lower marriage rates than comparable men who do not become fathers (see table 2.1).

Specifically, the annual marriage rate for unmarried fathers is only 76 percent that of other comparable unmarried men who did not have children. Not surprisingly, unmarried fathers also have much

**Table 2.1 Multivariate Cox Regression Results for Hazards Models Showing the Effects of Premarital Fatherhood on Risk of Union Formation of Black Men from the National Longitudinal Survey of Youth**

| | Dependent Variable | | | |
| --- | --- | --- | --- | --- |
| | Age at First Marriage | | Age at First Cohabitation | |
| Variable | B | $e^B$ | B | $e^B$ |
| Age at first nonmarital birth[a] | −.2657* | .7557 | .3965* | 1.4866 |
| Mother highest educational level | .0071 | 1.0072 | .0047 | 1.0047 |
| Man lived with two parents at age fourteen | .0085 | 1.0085 | −.0649 | .9372 |
| Urban-rural residence this year[a] | −.3167* | .7285 | .2541* | 1.2893 |
| Did child live with father this year?[a] | .5860* | 1.7968 | .3044* | 1.3558 |
| Man's education this year[a] | 0047 | 1.0047 | .1074* | 1.1134 |
| Weeks worked this year[a] | .5473* | 1.7286 | .1045 | 1.1101 |
| Arrested by age sixteen | −.0586 | .9431 | −.0262 | .9741 |
| Expelled or suspended from school by age sixteen | −.0463 | .9547 | .1232 | 1.1312 |
| Serious health problems by age sixteen | 0942 | 1.0987 | −.1668 | .8463 |
| Drank regularly as teen | −.1769 | .8379 | −.0704 | .9321 |
| Armed forces qualifying test percentile | .0053* | 1.0053 | −.0023 | .9977 |

*Source:* Author's compilation based on data from the NLSY, 1979 to 1993 waves.
[a]A time-varying covariate whose values may change in each year of the study.
N = 954                                    N = 1,021
−2 log likelihood = 6234.774*        −2 log likelihood = 6559.160*
*p ≤ .05

higher rates of cohabitation. Men who father children outside of marriage are 1.5 times more likely to cohabit than comparable men who do not become unmarried fathers. These equations are estimated with Cox Proportional Hazards Regressions. Such methods estimate the risk of an event—in this case, getting married, or starting to cohabit—as such risks are affected by other factors in the equation. For ease of understanding, the exponentiated regression coefficients ($e^B$) are also presented. Such coefficients indicate the change in risk associated with a unit change in the variable in question. For example, the first risk coefficient for marriage is .7557. This indicates that black men who had a child before marriage in the previous year have only about .76 the yearly risk of marriage of comparable black men who have not had a child. On the other hand, men who worked last year have higher chances of marriage as revealed by the coefficient for "weeks worked this year," 1.7286. The interpretation of these two equations is straightforward. Black men who had children before marriage have lower chances of getting married, and higher chances of cohabiting.

### Premarital Fatherhood and Achievement

To determine whether delayed or forgone marriage has predictable consequences for black men, four measures of adult achievement were analyzed to see how nonmarital fatherhood, marriage, and marital fatherhood affect each of them. These measures were total earnings in 1993, highest level of schooling obtained in 1993, weeks worked in 1992, and poverty status in 1993. The results are clear and convincing. The effects of nonmarital fatherhood on the measures of achievement in 1992 to 1993 are shown in table 2.2. These are average differences that have been adjusted for all the self-selection factors just mentioned.

Table 2.2  **Effects of Premarital Fatherhood on Adult Achievement: Results of Multivariate OLS and Logistic Regressions for Black Men from the National Longitudinal Survey of Youth**

|  | Earnings 1993 | Education 1993 | Weeks Worked 1992 | Poverty Status 1993 |
|---|---|---|---|---|
| Age at first premarital birth | B | B | B | Relative Risk |
| Fourteen to nineteen | −672 | −.340* | −3.508* | 1.615 |
| Twenty to twenty-five | −1,678* | −.257* | −0.897 | 1.389 |
| Twenty-six to thirty-five | −2,553* | −.253 | 2.771 | 1.882* |

*Source:* Author's compilation based on data from the NLSY, 1979 to 1993 waves.
*Note:* N = 1,355 black males; ordinary least squares and logistic regression. See table 2.1 results for controls.
*p < .05

To summarize these results, premarital fatherhood reduces men's earnings, educational attainments, and weeks worked. It increases the chances of poverty. These consequences vary somewhat, depending on the age at which a man first became a father.

The effects of premarital childbearing on men's lives are nuanced. Men who first became (unwed) fathers in their teens go on, ten to fourteen years later, to have annual incomes no different from men who never became unwed fathers (the value of –672 is not statistically significant). However, men who became unwed fathers later in life earn less. For example, those who first became unwed fathers in their early twenties earn $1,678 less than comparable men who never had a child. And men who first became unwed fathers in their late twenties earn $2,553 less than men who never had children outside of marriage. Men who first became unwed fathers as teenagers work an average of 3.5 weeks less per year than men who never became unwed fathers. Those who first become unwed fathers in their twenties, however, do not differ from other men in their labor-force attachment. On the other hand, early (teenage) fatherhood does not lead to higher rates of poverty later in life, whereas unmarried fatherhood at older ages (twenty-six and older) almost doubles the chances of poverty—it is 1.9 times greater

## MARRIAGE AND MARITAL BIRTHS

Marriage ameliorates many of the negative consequences of premarital fatherhood shown in table 2.2. More generally, marriage has significant positive consequences for most men, regardless of their fatherhood. And when the first child is born to a married couple, there are additional benefits for men. The results in table 2.3 show how much things change, on average, between the year before and the year after men experience a change in their marital status, and following the birth of their first child in marriage.

These results show that marriage brings about significant changes in income—$4,000 per year on average—and the birth of the first child has small additional effects (and income increase of $1,146 per year on average). The first marital birth carries enormous consequences for weeks worked (about five more weeks per year); marriage alone has smaller consequences for weeks worked (about two weeks more per year). Finally, marriage reduces the chances of poverty significantly, by a third of what they were before marriage,

Table 2.3  Consequences of Changes in Marital Status and First Marital Birth from Pooled Cross-Section Time Series with Fixed-Effects Models (Average Changes as a Result of Changes in Marital Status)

|  | Earnings | Education | Weeks Worked | Poverty Status |
|---|---|---|---|---|
| Change in marital status[a] |  |  |  |  |
| Marriage | 3,999* | .076* | 2.394* | 0.674* |
| Divorce | 788 | .184 | −.599 | 1.114 |
| Widowhood | −240 | .053 | −13.107* | 2.444* |
| Remarriage | −1,923 | 326 | −3.485* | 1.382* |
| First marital birth[b] | 1,146* | .421* | 4.782* | 0.973 |

*Source:* Author's compilation.
[a]Data from the NLSY, 1979 to 1993 waves. N = 1,610 black males; pooled, cross-section, time series with 18,729 person-years. All variables are time-varying covariates whose values may change yearly.
[b]Pooled, cross-section, time series with 3,229 married-person-years.
*p < .05.

though married fatherhood has no additional effect on the chances of poverty. The consequences of marriage and childbearing are trivial or insignificant for educational attainment.

## CONCLUSION

Conventional wisdom suggests that men are opposed to marriage, and that they marry only when a woman manages to convince them to. Perhaps this is so; perhaps not. Still, why would men avoid something that is so obviously beneficial?

In fact, men probably value and understand the benefits of marriage. Research shows that men fall in love faster and harder than women, that married men have better sex lives and are happier than bachelors, and that married men are healthier and live longer (Waite and Gallagher 2000). Are men unaware of such obvious benefits? Despite media portrayals of men as reluctant to marry, there is little evidence in support of such a view. Why do people believe that marriage is unwanted by men? Why do we continue to suggest that low marriage rates are a result of *men*'s unwillingness, or inability, to marry?

The answer, I believe, is that the institution of marriage is now being redefined in important and challenging ways. For the past four decades, marriage has been the object of much criticism, and possibly for good reason. The primary concern about marriage has been, and continues to be, its effects on women. Feminists typically believe that traditional marriage is incompatible with the expectations of modern women. In their public lives, women now live very differently than they did a few generations ago. In law, education, and the economy, barriers that restricted women's opportunities have been removed. We have enacted laws and policies that open doors that were traditionally closed to women. Public opinion surveys regularly show broad support for equality between the sexes in the public sphere. We are beginning to see women in roles once believed impossible or improper: senators, soldiers, lawyers, doctors, construction workers, engineers, and ministers. Public life has become much less gendered than it once was. But what about our private lives—in our families? How have these changes in women's lives been incorporated into our marriages?

An easy way to answer this question is to ask any young woman to compare her life options to those of her great-grandmother. On almost any important dimension, there are obvious and important differences. Women today may marry or remain single. They may pursue higher education, or not. They may have demanding careers. They can control their fertility.

Ask young men the same question, and the answers are very different but equally predictable. On almost every major dimension of life, men's options today are pretty much what they were three generations ago. So, in response to the question about how changes in women's lives have been incorporated into marriage, the answer is that they have not.

We are now in the later stages of a historic transformation. In half a century, what it means to be a woman, a wife, and a mother have been redefined. We have altered many non-family institutions in our society accordingly, but we have yet to incorporate these changes in women's lives into our understanding of *what a marriage is.*

Neither women nor men have fully adjusted to these changes in their married lives, even though they have adjusted to changes in public life, and perceive it as much less confusing. Marriage is challenging to men because the traditional assumptions about what it means to be a husband are no longer shared by the two sexes because wives are now actively involved in many of the same public (non-family) endeavors their husbands are. Disagreements about gender are nothing new. We have confronted them in law, business, education, politics, and religion, where gender battles have been waged openly, in public. All those institutions are different today than they were before such challenges were made, even if not uniformly (some conservative Protestant and most Catholic churches embrace rather traditional gender roles). The family is the last basic social institution to be confronted by these challenges about what it means to be a man, to be a woman.

Since marriage is so central to men's lives, we should not be surprised that it is confusing and challenging. How are couples to reconcile the new expectations for women with the traditional roles of men? Is marriage a part of women's adult lives? If so, what is a husband's appropriate role in a marriage? In fact, we have not yet resolved these questions. Every man and woman must confront these challenges with little guidance from tradition or convention. In short, a new model of marriage that incorporates the new gender realities has yet to be fully institutionalized.

The benefits of marriage and fatherhood are rarely central to debates about law and public policy. But the aggregate economic and social benefits that flow from marriage and fatherhood are clearly immense. Crafting a new model of marriage that will reconcile the public and private lives of men and women is not going to be easy, nor will it happen overnight. Most of the well-known family problems that have attracted attention in recent years—divorce, nonmarital childbearing, lower rates of marriage and increased cohabitation—are the costs we are paying to forge a new understanding of marriage. Those costs should not be minimized, for social change is always difficult, and changes in the meaning of marriage are particularly difficult to negotiate. Individual men and women may struggle with these matters and see them as purely personal problems. But many individuals' troubles cumulatively produce large social change by becoming defined as legitimate public issues. We are finally beginning to focus on the last, and most fundamental, institutions to be affected by the changing status of women: marriage and the family.

## REFERENCES

Anderson, Elijah. 1990. *Streetwise: Race, Class, and Change in an Urban Community.* Chicago: University of Chicago Press.

Lerman, Robert, and Theodora Ooms. 1993. *Young Unwed Fathers: Changing Roles and Emerging Policies.* Philadelphia: Temple University Press.

Moore, Kristin A. 1995. "Nonmarital Childbearing in the United States." In *Report to Congress on Out-of-Wedlock Childbearing*, U.S. Department of Health and Human Services, DHHS publication no. (PHS) 95-1257. Washington: U.S. Government Printing Office.

Nock, Steven L. 1998a. "The Consequences of Premarital Fatherhood." *American Sociological Review* 63(April): 250–63.

———. 1998b. *Marriage in Men's Lives*. New York: Oxford University Press.

Rowthorn, Robert. 2002. "Marriage as a Signal." In *The Law and Economics of Marriage and Divorce*, edited by Anthony W. Dnes and Robert Rowthorn. Cambridge: Cambridge University Press.

Sorensen, Elaine. 1998. "Nonresident Fathers: What Do We Know and What's Left to Learn?" Paper presented at the National Institute of Child Health and Human Development workshop, "Improving Data on Male Fertility and Family Formation." U.S. Department of Health and Human Service. Available at: *aspe.hhs.gov/search/fatherhood/htdocs/csforum/apenk.htm*.

U.S. Bureau of the Census. 1978. "Marital Status and Living Arrangements: March 1977." *Current Population Reports*, series P20, no. 323. Washington: U.S. Government Printing Office.

———. 1988. "Marital Status and Living Arrangements: March 1987." *Current Population Reports*, series P20, no. 423. Washington: U.S. Government Printing Office.

———. 1999. "Current Population Survey—1995." March supplement. Machine-readable computer file. Original untabulated data file available from the U.S. Bureau of the Census at: *www.bls.census.gov/cps/ads/adsmain.htm*.

———. 1998. "Marital Status and Living Arrangements: March 1997." *Current Population Reports*, series P20, no. 506. Washington: U.S. Government Printing Office.

———. 2000. "America's Families and Living Arrangements: March 2000." *Current Population Reports*, series P20, no. 537. Washington: U.S. Government Printing Office.

Waite, Linda J. 1995. Does Marriage Matter? *Demography* 32(4): 483–507.

Waite, Linda J., and Maggie Gallagher. 2000. *The Case for Marriage: Why Married People Are Happier, Healthier, and Better Off Financially*. New York: Doubleday.

Waite, Linda J., and Lee A. Lillard. 1991. "Children and Marital Disruption." *American Journal of Sociology* 96(4): 930–53.

Wilson, William Julius. 1980. *The Declining Significance of Race: Blacks and Changing American Institutions*. Chicago: University of Chicago Press.

———. 1990. *The Truly Disadvantaged: The Inner City, the Underclass, and Public Policy*. Chicago: University of Chicago Press.

# PART II

## Marriage from an Economic Perspective

# Chapter 3

## The Marriage Mystery: Marriage, Assets, and the Expectations of African American Families

### RONALD B. MINCY AND HILLARD POUNCY

Many people have noted that the out-of-wedlock birth rate of African Americans, 70 percent, is much higher than the rates for whites and Latinos (20 percent and 40 percent, respectively). This difference is so great that some—including some contributors to this volume—ask whether black fathers are necessary. In many cases, low-income black fathers themselves behave as if they did not believe they were necessary (Anderson 1999; Sullivan 1985, 1993). Such feelings seem to be less prevalent among their low-income white and Hispanic peers. In explaining high unwed birth rates within the African American community, some black fathers tell ethnographers that they cannot afford to "play house"—that is, operate as responsible fathers. Given the manner in which some black mothers behave, several studies have concluded that the mothers of these men's children also believe that black fathers are not necessary to their households (Wilson 1996, chapter 5; Patterson 1998; Edin 2000). Social policy in the United States functions as though policy makers, too, have concluded that black fathers may not be necessary. The welfare system is mainly geared to two types of families, neither of which involves fathers: those formed by divorce or widowhood, and those formed through out-of-wedlock pregnancy. The government laments high rates of unwed pregnancies but nonetheless provides support for single mothers and their children. In this way, the state seems to endorse the decision to keep fathers out. If behavior and policy speak loudly, then there is good reason to ask whether they are expressing the right views.

In response to high out-of-wedlock birth rates, fatherhood organizations led by persons of color—such as the National Center for Strategic Nonprofit Planning and Community Leadership and the

Center for Fathers, Families, and Public Policy—implicitly and sometimes explicitly suggest either that marriage is an unrealistic policy
goal for the African American community or that marriage is not
essential to effective fatherhood (Mincy 2001, 2002). Their positions
contrast with those taken by the Institute of American Values, whose
view is that fatherhood is most effective inside marriage (Gallagher
1999; Mincy and Pouncy 2001).

It turns out that African Americans have a comparative advantage
in creating wealth through marriage. Specifically, marriage significantly improves the economic well-being of black men. If black fathers
and black parents acted in accord with the contributions marriage
makes to their well-being, they would be the group most committed
to the institution of marriage. Paradoxically, however, if practitioners
serving African American fathers were to shift their positions and
advocate marriage to their clients, the consequences could be fatal to
their credibility and effectiveness, for cultural conditions and the practices of the nation's social service agencies have neutralized their ability to advocate marriage (Mincy and Pouncy 2001; Mincy 2002).

In this chapter we review the sources and studies on which the discussion of marriage is based; outline the magnitude of the problem;
review the evidence that marriage promotes child well-being; summarize the current state of the institution in the black community and
the meaning of these trends for black children; and examine the costs
and benefits of marriage for adults and the meaning of these data for
African American wealth creation. Last, we make some suggestions
as to how the context in which practitioners have to operate can be
changed and what steps they can take even under present circumstances to exploit the advantages marriage offers fathers, their children, and their families.

## MARRIAGE AND CHILD WELL-BEING

Does marriage promote child well-being? Black fatherhood groups
believe that the answer to this question is not so clear because studies
of the effects of marriage on child well-being compare children in married households only with their counterparts in divorced or separated
households. They do not compare children who begin life in non-
married households, the modal formation among African Americans,
with their counterparts who later experienced life in a married household. A married household formed after an out-of-wedlock birth can
be more troubled than an otherwise equivalent single-parent house-

hold (Edin 2000). In addition, single-parent households begun through an out-of-wedlock birth frequently evolve into households run by mature, competent, successful mothers (Stack 1974, Edin 2000). But it is also clear that low-income couples who marry may secure more help from relatives, especially from the father's side of the family.

In the aggregate, when demographers compare outcomes for children living with their biological parents in married households with their counterparts living in households with a divorced or separated parent, the former fare better than the latter. They are less likely to engage in risky behaviors such as becoming teenage parents or dropping out of high school. They are more likely to attend and complete college and to avoid idleness for extended periods after graduating from high school (McLanahan and Sandefur 1994).

Marriage offers several advantages. Married couples usually earn more than their divorced or never-married counterparts. In addition, a married couple is more likely to exercise effective supervision over and instill higher aspirations in their children. McLanahan and Sandefur estimate that the income advantage accounts for about half of the gains that children in married households show over children in divorced households. Another 40 percent can be attributed to higher levels of parental aspiration, more effective supervision, and greater involvement.

The fraction of children in two-parent households has been declining for several decades in all groups, but the decline has been especially noticeable among African American children.[1] In 1995 the proportion of black children living in two-parent households fell to a historic low of 33 percent, before rising to 36 percent in 1998. Much of the decline occurred in the 1970s: at the beginning of that decade a majority (58 percent) of black children lived in two-parent households, whereas a dozen years later the majority (54 percent) lived in single-parent households (see figure 3.1).

Although the proportion of white children living with two parents declined only slightly (from 90 percent in the 1960s to 83 percent by the late 1990s), the proportion of white children living with a single parent doubled. That figure rose from under 10 percent in the 1960s to just over 20 percent by the end of the 1990s. If this trend continues, within two decades the majority of white youth will live in single-parent households (see figure 3.2).

Declining marriage rates are a major reason that the number of children living in two-parent households has fallen, but there are complicating factors. The number of children living in cohabiting

## Figure 3.1 Living Arrangements of Black Children Under Age Eighteen, 1960 to 1998

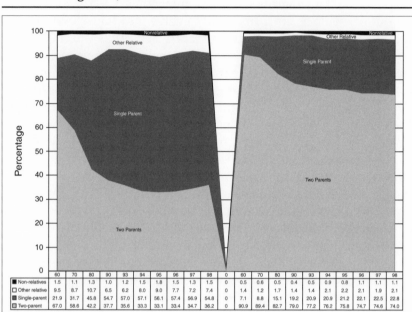

| | 60 | 70 | 80 | 90 | 93 | 94 | 95 | 96 | 97 | 98 | 0 | 60 | 70 | 80 | 90 | 93 | 94 | 95 | 96 | 97 | 98 |
|---|---|---|---|---|---|---|---|---|---|---|---|---|---|---|---|---|---|---|---|---|---|
| ■ Non-relatives | 1.5 | 1.1 | 1.3 | 1.0 | 1.2 | 1.5 | 1.8 | 1.5 | 1.3 | 1.5 | 0 | 0.5 | 0.6 | 0.5 | 0.4 | 0.5 | 0.9 | 0.8 | 1.1 | 1.1 | 1.1 |
| □ Other relative | 9.5 | 8.7 | 10.7 | 6.5 | 6.2 | 8.0 | 9.0 | 7.7 | 7.2 | 7.4 | 0 | 1.4 | 1.2 | 1.7 | 1.4 | 1.4 | 2.1 | 2.2 | 2.1 | 1.9 | 2.1 |
| ■ Single-parent | 21.9 | 31.7 | 45.8 | 54.7 | 57.0 | 57.1 | 56.1 | 57.4 | 56.9 | 54.8 | 0 | 7.1 | 8.8 | 15.1 | 19.2 | 20.9 | 20.9 | 21.2 | 22.1 | 22.5 | 22.8 |
| □ Two-parent | 67.0 | 58.6 | 42.2 | 37.7 | 35.6 | 33.3 | 33.1 | 33.4 | 34.7 | 36.2 | 0 | 90.9 | 89.4 | 82.7 | 79.0 | 77.2 | 76.2 | 75.8 | 74.7 | 74.6 | 74.0 |

*Source:* Authors' configuration based on Joint Center for Political and Economic Studies, Census Current Population Reports (1960 to 1998).

## Figure 3.2 Percentage of Children Under Eighteen Living Below the Poverty Level, 1977 to 1997

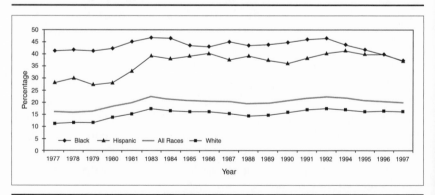

*Source:* Authors' configuration based on Joint Center for Political and Economic Studies, Census Current Population Reports (1977 to 1997).

households has increased,[2] and in the short term this trend offsets declines attributable to marital dissolution or other types of single-parent household formations. In the longer term, any compensatory effects linked to cohabitation evaporate, because cohabiting unions are less stable than marital unions. Thus it is important to understand why marriage is in decline.

The sources of marital decline—an increase in the number of marriages that end in divorce, a higher number of widows and widowers, and an increase in the number of individuals who never marry—vary by race. The proportion of married African American men over age fifteen fell from 64 percent in 1950 to 41.6 percent in 1998—a decrease largely attributable to a growth in the numbers of those who never married and who divorced. In 1950, 28 percent of African American men never married, as compared with 46.2 percent in 1998 (see figure 3.3). The proportion of divorced African American males rose from 2 percent in 1950 to 9.1 percent in 1998. The slight declines in marriage among white males (67 percent were married in 1950, and 60 percent in 1998) are largely attributable to divorce (a rise from 2 percent in 1950 to 8.3 percent in 1998). The proportion of unmarried

**Figure 3.3  Marital Status of American Men, 1950 to 1998**

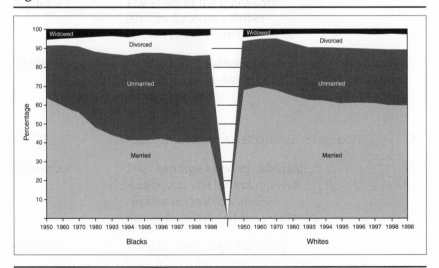

*Source:* Authors' configuration based on Joint Center for Political and Economic Studies, Census Current Population Reports (1950 to 1998).

white males increased only slightly, from 26 percent in 1950 to 29 percent in 1998.

There have been similar changes among black women (see figure 3.4).

The proportion of married African American women fell from 62 percent to 37 percent between 1950 and 1998, while the decline for white women was from 66 percent to 57 percent. Divorce trends have been comparable between the races, with the divorce rate increasing from 3 percent to 12 percent among black women and from 2 percent to 11 percent among white women. Between 1950 and 1998 the percentage of never-married black women doubled, from 21 percent to 41 percent, whereas the corresponding percentage among white women remained virtually flat, from 20 percent in 1950 to 22 percent by 1998.

Perhaps the most telling trends are those of increasing inequality across family types. Between 1960 and the late 1990s median family income grew by 27 percent for black families and 30 percent for white families (see figure 3.5).

**Figure 3.4  Marital Status of American Women, 1950 to 1998**

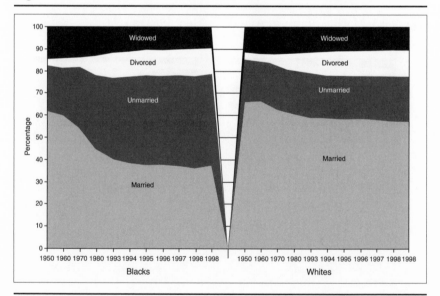

*Source:* Authors' configuration based on Joint Center for Political and Economic Studies, Census Current Population Reports (1950 to 1998).

**Figure 3.5  Median Income of Black Families by Selected Types
Compared to White Couples, 1967 to 1998**

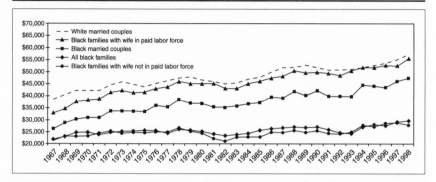

*Source:* Authors' configuration based on Joint Center for Political and Economic
Studies, Census Current Population Reports (1967 to 1998).

Married black couples, however, were responsible for much of
the increase among blacks. Among married black couples median
income grew by 73 percent, whereas it grew at a much more modest
37 percent for married white couples. This obviously had a strong
impact on child poverty. In the 1990 census, only 9 percent of children
in two-parent families lived below the poverty line, as compared with
almost half of children in mother-only households (Farley 1998, 123)
(for child poverty outcomes by race see figure 3.2).

Racial and ethnic variations in child living standards may also
result from racial and ethnic differences in child-support payments.
Elaine Sorensen (1995) has calculated that if all nonresident fathers
nationwide paid Wisconsin's standard child-support levels, they
would generate $44 billion to $48 billion in child-support revenues
versus the $14 billion to $15 billion currently collected. She also shows
that almost two-thirds of nonresident white fathers, one-third of nonresident Hispanic fathers, and less than one-third of nonresident black
fathers pay some child support (see figure 3.6). Given that earnings
and employment rates exhibit a similar rank order by race, it is possible that variations in the child-support contributions of nonresident
fathers simply reflect variations in ability to pay.

Marriage promotes child well-being, but children are dependent
and cannot on their own secure the benefits of a married household.
Does marriage offer enough advantages to adults to motivate them to

**Figure 3.6  Percent of Nonresident Dads in Three Racial-Ethnic Groups Who Pay Child Support**

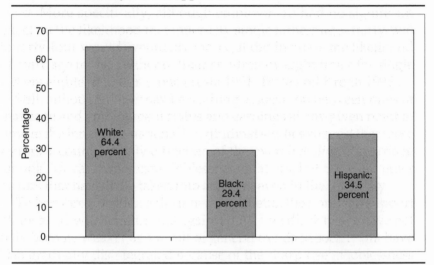

*Source:* Authors' calculations based on Survey of Income Program Participation (1990).

marry and remain married so that the interests of their children are also secured?

### MARRIAGE AND ADULT WELL-BEING

Calculating how much a couple secures from marriage involves two separate calculations—a calculation of direct gains and a calculation of indirect gains. A married person benefits directly from marriage when he or she earns more than a cohabiting or single counterpart. A married person benefits indirectly from marriage when his or her earnings and his or her spouse's earnings secure for him or her a household income greater than the household income of his or her cohabiting equivalent. In a single-earner couple, for example, the working partner might secure a higher direct gain (higher earnings than an unmarried peer) but a lower indirect gain (household income) than an unmarried peer in a two-earner cohabiting relationship. In another example, the nonworking partner in a single-earner household might secure a lower direct gain from marriage (no job, hence no earnings) than his or her unmarried (single) peer but a higher indirect gain (higher household income) than his or her unmarried counterpart. If a married woman has lower earnings than her cohabiting counterpart, then, with all else held equal, the indirect gain from marriage (household income) for that married woman's spouse is smaller than for the cohabiting woman's partner. The indirect gain from marriage reflects the married person's individual contribution plus the higher family income gained when each spouse shares with his or her partner.

Let us focus on the direct gains obtained through marriage. Using data from the Census Bureau's *Current Population Survey*, which began to include data on cohabiting couples only in 1995, Philip Cohen (1999, 2000) examined the relative financial advantages of marriage and cohabitation among a sample of adults between twenty-four and fifty-four years old who earned at least two dollars per hour, on average, for a year. Focusing on returns between 1995 and 1997, he found that married men earn significantly more than never-married men, cohabiting men, and formerly married men (divorced, separated, or widowed). More specifically, when Cohen controlled for number of children, education, work experience, and region of the country, he found that married white, black, and Hispanic men earn 22, 18, and 15 percent, respectively, more than their never-married white, black, and Hispanic counterparts (see figure 3.7, in which log-wage differences are a proxy for percentage differences). As figure 3.7 indicates, married men earn between 6 and 11 percent more than cohabiting men; the larger gains go to white, black, and Hispanic men, in that order.

The role of selection bias in the association between marriage and increased earnings for men remains unclear. By selection bias, researchers mean some unobservable factor, like dependability, that is positively correlated with earnings and the likelihood that individuals marry. Steven L. Nock, for example (see chapter 2, this volume), once compared the earnings of married and never-married brothers to control for selection bias and determined that the gains to marriage were still large and significant. Though siblings are a weak control for selection bias, in subsequent work Nock, Linda Waite, and several other demographers, using a variety of methods to control for selection bias, commonly find significant support for an independent, or productivity effect of marriage on men's earnings. (Discussion summarized in Waite, 2000.)[3] Nevertheless, Christopher Cornwell and Peter Rupert (1997) show that estimates of this independent effect fall precipitously when detailed controls for men's characteristics are included in the model. This suggests that selection bias could be substantial in studies lacking detailed characteristics of men.

**Figure 3.7  Log-Wage Difference of Married from Never Married, by Race-Ethnicity and Gender, 1994 to 1996**

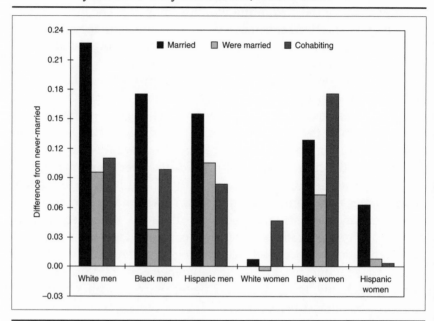

*Source:*  Cohen (1999), reprinted with permission; U.S. Census Bureau (1994–1996).

Cohen's findings on the direct gains of marriage for women are mixed. For both black and white women, cohabitation brings greater gains than marriage. Cohabiting white women earn 5 percent more than their never-married counterparts, whereas married white women earn only 1 percent more than their never-married counterparts. Cohabiting black women earn almost 18 percent more than their never-married counterparts, whereas married black women earn 13 percent more than their never-married peers. In contrast, married Hispanic women earn 6 percent more than their never-married counterparts, but for Hispanic women the gains from cohabitation are negligible.

Findings on the indirect gains acquired through marriage vary by gender. Direct gains are positive for men of all racial and ethnic groups, so indirect gains are also positive for women of all race and ethnic groups. That is, married women live in households with higher incomes than cohabiting or never-married women, because the former benefit from their husband's earnings premiums (Waite 2000;

Landry 2000). By the same logic, the second component is negative for men (except for Hispanics), because cohabiting women earn more than married women.

Despite these mixed results for indirect gains, the net effect is that married people have the highest household incomes. Married blacks earned 31 percent more than their never-married counterparts, and cohabiting blacks earned 37 percent more than their never-married counterparts (sums of married columns and of cohabiting columns in figure 3.7). Married whites earned 23 percent more than their never-married counterparts, and cohabiting whites earned 14 percent more than their never-married counterparts. That is, although the indirect gains are negative for men, the direct gains are so large relative to the wage premium of cohabiting women that the net effect is that married men have higher incomes than cohabiting or never-married men. This is also true for married women. Even though cohabiting women earn more than married women on average, a husband's earnings premium is so large that it offsets the cohabiting women's earning premium. The net effect is that married women on average have higher household incomes than cohabiting or never-married women.

Even if married and cohabiting couples earned the same level of income, married couples would be better off. The reason is that married couples pool their resources with greater freedom, raising the level of consumption they derive from their incomes. Cohabiting couples, by contrast, are more likely to hold separate savings and checking accounts, which indicates that their income pooling is more constrained than that of married couples (Brines and Joyner 1999). But married and cohabiting couples do not earn the same amount; married couples earn more.

## HOUSEHOLDS COMPARED BY RACE

Marriage increases the economic well-being of children and adults of all races. A further question is: Does marriage reflect, amplify, or reduce racial inequality? Some differences in how black and white marriages operate are a consequence of inequality, and marriage does amplify inequality. In other respects, it abates inequality, and marriage can conceivably overcome inequality or even reverse racial inequality.

As a consequence of long-standing inequality, married African Americans have shown a greater commitment to building dual-earner, married households than their white counterparts.[4] Until recently, the employment decisions of white wives were likely to be most related to the economic need of their households and the presence of young children. The employment decisions of black wives are inversely related to the economic need of their households, and the presence of children had less impact on their employment decisions. Thus, in comparing households by race, the main difference between the groups rests in the employment decision of wives.

At the midpoint of the twentieth century the majority of middle-class black wives worked. Before World War II almost 40 percent of married middle-class African American women were in the labor force, compared with 15 percent of married middle-class white women. After the war the proportion of dual-earner couples increased in both groups. By the 1970s 70 percent of married middle-class African American wives worked. By contrast, in the 1970s fewer than 50 percent of white married middle-class women worked. After the 1990s, racial gaps between dual-earner couples have increasingly narrowed, so that the difference between the groups was less than 10 percent (85 percent of middle-class black wives and 77 percent of middle-class white wives were employed).

Bart Landry (2000) and the historian Jacqueline Jones (1985) sketch out some of the reasons that African Americans adopted the dual-earner household, termed the "modern family," so early.[5] During Reconstruction, married African American women were subject to coercive labor policies mandating that all African African women work "for their own good." Similarly, African American sharecropper families were subject to customary, informal arrangements according to which a married woman's time belonged to the landlord's household, her own farm, her household, and then herself, in that order. Both blacks and whites valued households with breadwinner fathers and stay-at-home mothers, but a lasting consequence of life in the rural South and racial discrimination in the industrial North was a greater willingness on the part of African Americans to consider dual-earner arrangements in their repertoire of household formations.[6]

Despite the tendency of married African Americans to form two-earner households, in one critical respect marriage perpetuates racial inequality. When compared in terms of wealth—defined as accumulated assets and access to resources or, more specifically, net assets minus debt—marriage may increase inequality. When Melvin Oliver and Thomas Shapiro (1995) compared black and white middle-class married households, they found large gaps in the net worth of such couples. Black married couples earned 80 percent of the income of their white counterparts but held only 27 percent of their white equivalents' net worth. Similarly, black two-earner couples earned 85 percent of the income of their white counterparts and held only 31 percent of their white counterparts' net worth. These net-worth gaps were larger among two-earner young couples and white-collar couples. (Young black two-earner couples held 18 percent of their white counterparts' net worth. Black couples employed in white-collar jobs held 16 percent of their white counterparts' net worth.) Because there are few marriages across American racial boundaries, the institution of marriage acts to maintain the nation's substantial wealth inequalities by race.

Traditionally, scholars have softened the view that marriage perpetuates large wealth gaps between the races by noting that marriage also acts to abate inequality, in that marriage at least allows blacks to approach the living standard of white families (Oliver and Shapiro 1995). That is, dual-earner married households give blacks entry into the middle class. However, recent research suggests that for blacks the relationship between middle- and upper-middle-class status and dual-earner households may be more complex than originally thought. For blacks, dual-earner households may be a consequence as much as a "cause" of class.

Landry observes that black wives with "no real economic need to work" were more likely to work than women who do have a real need to work. He interprets this as evidence of the presence of a group consciousness or ideology committing the group to the modern family for the past century.

> The work decisions of upper-middle-class wives are, I believe, powerful indicators of the force of competing domestic ideologies. Because these women are married to men who earn the highest incomes of all workers—professional men and men in management—they have no real economic need to work. Their decision to work can therefore be viewed as flowing more directly from their beliefs about their proper roles than the work decisions of women in other classes, who are likely to be influenced also by economic need. . . . If economic need is the primary motivation for the entrance of wives into the labor force, we should find a higher proportion of lower- than upper-middle-class married women at work outside the home. (Landry 2000, 102)

Until recently, we were more likely to see dual-earner white couples than African American couples exhibiting the pattern Landry ascribes to economic need—that is, a higher proportion of lower- than upper-middle-class married women at work outside the home. From the 1940s until the 1980s, white lower-middle-class wives with children were more likely to be employed than their upper-middle-class counterparts. Employment rates for lower-middle-class white wives grew from 12 percent in the 1940s to 50 percent in 1980. During the same period employment rates for upper-middle-class white wives lagged by about ten percentage points behind those for lower-middle-class white women. Since the 1980s the gap between lower- and upper-middle-class white households has closed as whites encounter some of the factors that had affected African Americans in the century's first quarter: namely, well-educated women developed an ideology endorsing their opportunity to work outside the home at the same time as male earnings declined. This latter factor made dual-earner households more a necessity than a personal choice.

By contrast, over the same period black upper-middle-class wives were more likely to work than their lower-middle-class counterparts. From the 1940s to the 1990s employment rates among upper-middle-class married African American women grew from 40 percent to almost 90 percent. In the same period employment rates among lower-middle-class black wives grew from almost 30 percent in 1940 to over 80 percent by the 1990s.

Finally, when the presence of children, particularly young children, is taken into account, the rate at which upper-middle-class black wives participate in the labor force converges with that of their black childless counterparts. This convergence is greater than for upper-middle-class white wives with children and their white childless counterparts. In 1960, after a husband's income and a wife's education were taken into account, middle-class African American wives aged twenty-five to forty-four with children were 66 percent less likely to work than middle-class African American wives with a similar background but without children. In the 1990s a black middle-class wife with children was only 20 percent less likely to work than her counterpart without children. By contrast, in the 1960s middle-class white wives with children were 80 percent less likely to work than their childless counterparts, and by the 1990s this was still

70 percent less likely. Landry calculates that this difference by race in how middle-class wives respond to the presence of children largely reflects changes in the behavior of black middle-class wives with preschool children over the last forty years. Whereas 50 percent of black wives were employed in the 1950s, almost 90 percent of them were working by the 1990s.

In summary, unlike their white counterparts, high-earning black males were likely to marry high-earning black females (Zimmer 1996). High-earning white males tend to be paired with low-earning females. High-earning Hispanic males tend to be paired with low-earning females, but the process also "unites [Hispanic] males who work longer hours with females who do the same." In addition, when black males earn enough to achieve a middle-income household with one salary—and thus could operate a traditional household—the women in those households not only work but are likely to contribute a significant portion of the family's income.

## THE MODERN FAMILY AND FISCAL PARITY

A side effect of a strong commitment to the modern family is fiscal parity between husbands and wives. This factor plays an especially significant role for African Americans. African American marriages exhibit smaller earnings gaps between husband and wife than is true of other groups (see figures 3.8 and 3.9).

Since the 1980s the earnings gap between husband and wife in over half of black marriages has been $10,000 or less (see figure 3.8). In some instances wives earned more than husbands. In the same period the proportion of black wives whose earnings exceeded their husband's by more than $10,000 doubled, from 8 percent to 17 percent. In an earlier period—1976 to 1983, when male earnings nationally first declined sharply (see Bound and Holzer 1991)—the proportion of black husbands who earned $10,000 or more than their wives fell by 10 percent, from a high of 58 percent in 1976 to 48 percent by 1983. By the late 1990s the gap between a husband's and wife's earnings was less than $10,000 in almost one-third of African American marriages.

Similar dynamics were at work among white married households but did not yield similar levels of domestic parity. Since the 1980s in

**Figure 3.8  Relative Earnings of Wife and Husband in Black Married Couples, 1976 to 1999**

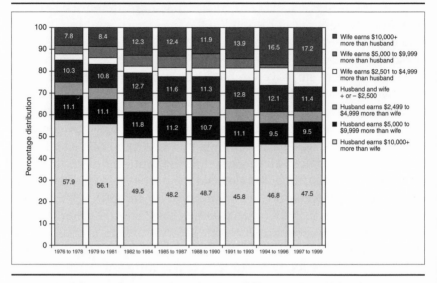

Source: Authors' configuration based on March Current Population Surveys (1976 to 1999), with assistance from Philip Cohen.
Note: Non-Hispanic civilian couples with at least one earner (based on wife's race).

**Figure 3.9  Relative Earnings of Wife and Husband in White Married Couples, 1976 to 1999**

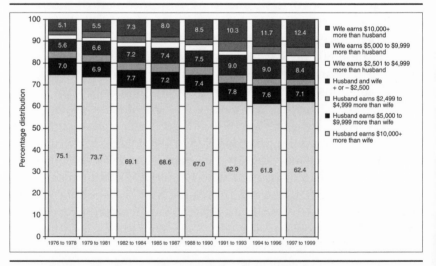

Source: Authors' configuration based on March Current Population Surveys (1976 to 1999) with assistance from Philip Cohen.
Note: Non-Hispanic civilian couples with at least one earner (based on wife's race).

a substantial majority of white married households the gap between the husband's and wife's earnings has been more than $10,000. That majority ranged from two-thirds of marriages in the 1980s to three-fifths in the 1990s. Meanwhile, the proportion of white wives whose earnings exceeded their husband's by more than $10,000 also doubled, from 5.5 percent to 12.4 percent. In a single decade (1978 to 1988) the proportion of marriages in which the husband earned $10,000 or more in excess of the wife's earnings fell from three-quarters (75.1 percent) to two-thirds (67 percent). Nonetheless, by the late 1990s, in the majority (over 60 percent) of white married households the husband still outearned the wife by $10,000 or more.

Because figures 3.8 and 3.9 conflate all married couples, they obscure differences among couples by number of children, levels of education, and proportions of dual-earning households. When we take these factors into account, slight residual differences in fiscal parity remain (see figure 3.10).

Among modern families with children present, African American wives at all educational levels have contributed 50 percent or more of family earnings since the mid-1990s. From the late 1970s until the mid-1990s, well-educated African American wives (defined as wives with some college or more) were closest in parity to their husbands, providing at least 40 percent of family income. In the 1980s they provided at least 45 percent of family income, and in the late 1990s they provided 50 percent. Less well-educated African American wives with children in modern families contributed 35 percent of family income in the 1970s. Their contributions averaged 40 percent in the 1980s. In the 1990s their contributions to family earnings were the highest of all groups tabulated in figure 3.10: 50 percent by the middle of the 1990s, and a majority by the last half of that decade.

In the last twenty-five years white working wives with children in modern households at all educational levels doubled their contributions to household earnings. The contributions of well-educated white working wives with children now approach those of their black counterparts, but significant gaps still remain between less well-educated white working wives with children and their black counterparts. Twenty-five years ago, white working wives with children at all educational levels contributed less than a quarter of family income. By the end of the 1980s well-educated white working wives with children contributed a third of family earnings, and their less well-educated counterparts contributed less than 30 percent. By the end of the 1990s

**Figure 3.10  Fiscal Parity by Race and Education Among Dual-Earner Married Couples with Children**

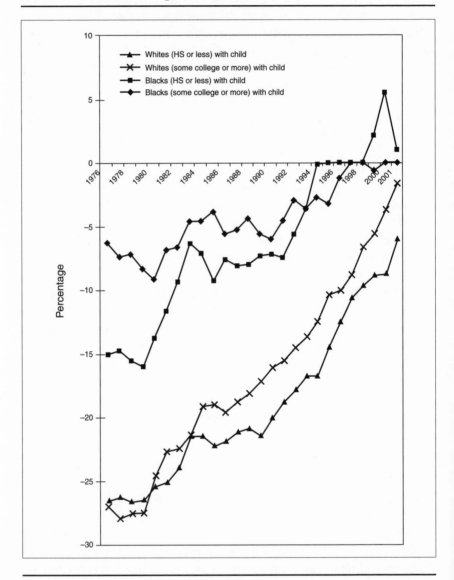

*Source:* Authors' configuration based on data from the March Current Population Survey (1976 to 2001), prepared with assistance of the Joint Center for Political and Economic Studies.
*Note:* At 0 percent, a wife's share equals a husband's share. At less than 0 percent, a wife's share is less than a husband's share. At greater than 0 percent, a wife's share is greater than a husband's share.

well-educated working mothers with children contributed 48 percent of family earnings, and less well-educated married mothers contributed over 40 percent.

Another way to appreciate the greater commitment of black wives to work is to observe what happens to these wives in the presence of children. One way to assess how much black and white modern families have converged in the last twenty-five years without losing sight of the residual differences by race is to ask what happens when a working wife has children and keeps working. We already know that middle-class African American working wives are disproportionately likely to return to work after having a child. What happens to fiscal parity when working wives return to work after children join the household? Do they contribute less after having children, or does it make any difference? Or, improbably, do they contribute more to household income? In figure 3.11 we imagine the effect of children on a wife's share of family earnings after taking into account education and race. Ideally, we might also take into account the quality of child care available to these mothers and their husbands' earnings. Then we would be able to observe a panel of families over time, before and after they had children.

In the 1990s well-educated black working wives with children contributed 10 percent less than well-educated working wives who did not have children, but typically their share of family earnings was within 5 percent of that of their childless counterparts. Until the 1990s children did affect how much a less well-educated black mother contributed to her household; they were typically associated with declines of up to 25 percent in the share of family earnings contributed by women in this group. Since the 1990s the presence of children has not had much effect on a less well-educated black mother's share of earnings.

In the last twenty-five years the change in a mother's share of earnings among well-educated white wives has been dramatic. In the late 1970s well-educated white working mothers contributed almost half of what their counterparts without children contributed. By the late 1990s the difference between the two was negligible. A similar shift took place among less well-educated white mothers. In the late 1970s less well-educated white working mothers contributed 35 percent less than their counterparts without children. By the late 1990s the gap between the two was still 10 percent—the largest remaining gap observed between working wives with and without children.

## Figure 3.11  Effect of Children on Wife's Share of Family Earnings by Wife's Education and Race (Dual-Earner Households)

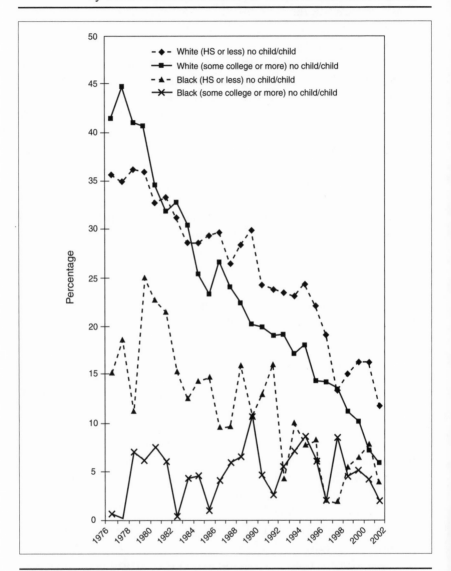

*Source:* Authors' configuration based on March Current Population Surveys (1976 to 2001), prepared with the assistance of the Joint Center for Political and Economic Studies.
*Note:* Each trend line is a ratio such that the share of family earnings for a wife with children is in the denominator, and the share of family earnings for a wife without children is in the numerator. As the ratio approaches zero, a wife with one or more children contributes as much to family earnings as a wife with no children, implying that the presence of children has had no effect on a wife's earnings for that racial group at that education level.

Given these outcomes, there is a concern that the African American commitment to the modern household may be so strong that the well-being of black children is jeopardized. Black working wives who have had children return to full-time work significantly faster than their white counterparts, and this is especially true of women in income brackets where economic necessity is less likely to be a factor in their decision. However, most recent studies on the effects of a mother's employment on child well-being conclude that there is a cost to young children when their mothers work full-time (Landry 2000).

Finally, African American marriages could conceivably overcome or even reverse racial inequality in this respect. When black and white men of similar educational backgrounds do finally earn equal pay, the employment decision of black wives should earn the black couple greater incomes. In that sense, marriage would offer African Americans an income creation advantage over their white counterparts.

This section has shown that the gains to marriage for African Americans are substantial—which only deepens the question, "Why is marriage such a troubled institution in two respects, the low rates of initiation and the high rates of dissolution?"

## THE MARRIAGE MYSTERY

Historically, African Americans have based their marriages on fiscal parity. As a result, African American men and children in married families are better off than their unmarried counterparts, and African American married women are better off than their single (non-cohabiting) counterparts. So, why are divorce rates among African Americans so high? Why are so many African Americans never-married? Fiscal parity poses risks for the institution of marriage among African Americans. It is more difficult to maintain relationships based on fiscal parity (Brines and Joyner 1999; Cohen 2000). Therefore, African Americans are more likely to divorce. Unions based on fiscal parity are more stable when the parity is maintained. This exposes African American marriages to a double risk: one arises when one of the partners loses a job; the other arises when one of the partners experiences a significant increase in income.

Although it increases the risk of divorce, fiscal parity may also be a pre-requisite for marriage. African American women are more likely than their white or Hispanic peers to expect their male partner to have an adequate income before marriage (Tucker 1995). Given the dynamics of modern families, it is reasonable to assume that African American men hold similar expectations of their partners. Just as evenly yoked couples must negotiate the perils of maintaining parity after marriage, similar dynamics may be at work before marriage. Both prospective marriage partners must meet the expectations of parity (Edin 2000; Wilson 1996).[7]

Finally, low-income African Americans idealize and prize marriage so much that they have established a pecking order in which having a child is first, having a relationship is second, and marrying is likely only under the "right" circumstances (Edin 2000; Mincy and Huang 2002).

Current social welfare policies may create barriers to family maintenance or even family formation among blacks because these policies assist low-skilled black women (mothers) in their attempts to leave welfare, find employment, and increase wages. However, low-skilled black men receive much less, much less organized, and much less effective assistance in their attempts to increase employment and earnings. This makes it difficult for low-skilled black men to achieve and maintain fiscal parity with their potential marriage partners.

---

We gratefully acknowledge the invaluable assistance of Philip Cohen of the University of California, Irvine, and Roderick Harrison of Howard University, who heads the Data Bank Project at the Joint Center for Political and Economic Studies in Washington, D.C. We also thank Cassandra Cassave of the Data Bank Project, Belinda Tucker, Steven Nock, Sara McLanahan, Flona Mincy, Elaine Sorensen, Eric Rhodes, and an anonymous reader for useful comments and references.

## NOTES

1. Data from the 2000 census, not incorporated into this discussion, show hopeful increases in the proportion of children in two-parent married and cohabiting households, which appear to reverse this trend (Dupree and Primus 2001).

2. Without indicating how many of these unions include children, Bumpass and Lu (1999) report a 20 percent increase in cohabitation among women in their thirties between 1987 and 1995. In 1995 almost half of women in this age group had cohabited outside marriage, versus 40 percent in 1987. In 1995 almost a quarter of never-married women were cohabiting at the time they were interviewed, versus 15 percent in 1987. Like the overall decline

in marriage, cohabitation accounts for a larger portion of the decline in marriage for blacks than for whites (Bumpass, Sweet, and Cherlin 1991).

3. There is little consensus on why marriage has such large independent effects on male earnings. Steven Nock (Nock 1998) speculates that marriage exposes men to the expectations of in-laws and signals compliant behavior to employers. David Blankenhorn (1995) suggests that marriage "socializes" or "civilizes" men perhaps resulting in wage gains. However, it is also clear that when married women work they, too, benefit from productivity effects (Cohen, Gray, and Vanderhart 2000, 366). This implies that whatever marriage does for male earnings, it could do for female earnings as well. Arlie Hochschild (1989) comments that although this is a possibility, in practice the efficiencies and bargains of marriage are rarely structured to benefit working wives as much as working husbands.

4. This section's discussion is largely based upon recent work by Bart Landry (2000) and his thesis that the employment decisions of black wives are inversely related to economic need. He suggests that class is an important variable in considering variation in the commitment of blacks and whites to modern families. Landry defines class by occupation. In an upper-middle-class household at least one adult works in a managerial or professional occupation. In a lower-middle-class household the adult with the highest-ranking occupation works in sales or has a clerical job.

5. Preindustrial and "modern family" types bracket the traditional family in that both feature spouses who co-locate their work—both work in the home or both work outside the home. In the preindustrial household both spouses worked at home. In the modern household both work away from the house. In the late nineteenth and early twentieth centuries, as other groups intensified their attachment to the traditional family, in which only the husband works outside the home, African Americans—particularly upper-middle-class African American women—idealized the modern family and made it their specialty. To a certain extent they pioneered the modern dual-earner, even the dual-career, "power" couple.

6. In a revealing parallel, a half-century after Reconstruction ended in this country, the Soviet Union promoted similar goals. The state "outlawed" the housewife and undermined the "male prerogative within the family" through legislation and coercion, as the American slavery system had done to African American males. Specifically, the Soviet state "assumed responsibility for the fulfillment of the traditional masculine roles of father and provider, becoming, in effect, a universal patriarch to which both men and women were subject" (Ashwin 2002, 23). After the Soviet Union collapsed, "[T]he position of housewife was ideologically rehabilitated, so that women theoretically now face a choice over whether or not to work." As happened in the United States (particularly among African Americans), the modern family is now the norm in Russia; and when in

post-Soviet society men perceive a choice between providing for a family and maintaining "public status," they choose the latter (Ashwin 2002).

7. There is a well-known race effect in comparative studies of marriage and family formation. Among whites marriage rates are highly correlated with female earnings. The higher the wife's earnings, the lower are white marriage rates. Such patterns are muted among blacks, and Robert Lerman has noted that even "marriageable" middle- and higher-income black males are less likely to marry than their white and Hispanic peers (Lerman 1989).

## REFERENCES

Anderson, Elijah. 1999. *Code of the Street: Decency, Violence, and the Moral Life of the Inner City*. New York: W.W. Norton.

Ashwin, S. 2002. "The Influence of the Soviet Gender Order on Employment Behavior in Contemporary Russia." *Sociological Research* 41(1): 21–37.

Blankenhorn, David. 1995. *Fatherless America: Confronting Our Most Urgent Social Problem*. New York: Basic Books.

Bound, John, and Harry Holzer. 1991. "Industrial Shifts, Skill Levels, and the Labor Market for White and Black Males." Population Studies Center research report no. 91-211. Ann Arbor: University of Michigan.

Brines, J., and K. Joyner. 1999. "The Ties That Bind: Principles of Cohesion in Cohabitation and Marriage." *American Sociological Review* 64(3): 333–55.

Bumpass, Larry, J. A. Sweet, and A. Cherlin. 1991. "The Role of Cohabitation in Declining Rates of Marriage." *The Journal of Marriage and the Family* 53(November): 913–27.

Bumpass, Larry, and H. H. Lu. 1999. "Trends in Cohabitation and Implications for Children's Family Contexts in the United States." *Population Studies: A Journal of Demography* 54(March): 29–41.

Cohen, Philip N. 1999. "Racial-Ethnic and Gender Differences in Returns to Cohabitation and Marriage: Evidence from the Current Population Survey." U.S. Bureau of the Census, Population Division, working paper no. 35. Washington: Government Printing Office.

———. 2000. "Cohabitation, Marriage, and Earnings: Racial-Ethnic and Gender Differences, 1995–1998." Manuscript.

———. 2002. "Cohabitation and the Declining Marriage Premium for Men." *Work and Occupations* 29(3): 341–63.

Cornwell, Christopher, and Peter Rupert. 1997. "Unobservable Individual Effects, Marriage and the Earnings of Young Men." *Economic Inquiry*. XXXV(April): 285–94.

Dupree, A., and W. Primus. 2001. "Declining Share of Children Lived with Single Mothers in the Late 1990s: Substantial Differences by Race and Income." Report. Washington, D.C.: Center on Budget and Policy Priorities.

Edin, Kathryn. 2000. "What Do Low-income Single Mothers Say about Marriage?" *Social Problems* 47(February): 112–33.

Farley, Reynolds. 1998. *The New American Reality: Who We Are, How We Got Here, Where We Are Going.* New York: Russell Sage Foundation.

Gallagher, Maggie. 1999. "The Importance of Being Married." In *The Fatherhood Movement,* edited by Wade Horn, David Blankenhorn, Mitch Pearlstein, and Don Eberley. Lanham, Md.: Lexington Books.

Gray, Jeffrey S., and Michael J. Vanderhart. 2000. "On the Determination of Wages: Does Marriage Matter?" In *The Ties That Bind: Perspectives on Marriage and Cohabitation,* edited by Linda Waite. New York: Walter de Gruyter.

Hochschild, Arlie Russell. 1989. *The Second Shift.* New York: Viking Penguin.

Jones, Jaqueline. 1985. *Labor of Love, Labor of Sorrow: Black Women, Work and the Family from Slavery to the Present.* New York: Vintage Books.

Landry, Bart. 2000. *Black Working Wives: Pioneers of the American Family Revolution.* Berkeley: University of California Press.

Lerman, Robert I. 1989. "Employment Opportunities of Young Men and Family Formation." *American Economic Review Papers and Proceedings* 79: 62–66.

McLanahan, Sara, and Gary Sandefur. 1994. *Growing Up with a Single Parent: What Hurts, What Helps.* Cambridge, Mass.: Harvard University Press.

Mincy, Ronald. 2001. "Marriage, Child Poverty, and Public Policy." *American Experiment Quarterly* 4(2): 68–71.

———. 2002. "What About Black Fathers?" *The American Prospect* 13(7): 56–8.

Mincy, Ronald, and A. Dupree. 2001. "Welfare, Child Support, and Family Formation." *Children's and Youth Services Review* 23(6–7): 577–601.

Mincy, Ronald, and Chien-Chung Huang. 2002. " 'Just Get Me to the Church . . .': Assessing Policies to Promote Marriage Among Fragile Families." Working paper no. 02-02-February. Center for Research on Child Well-being, Princeton University.

Mincy, Ronald, and Hillard Pouncy. 1997. "Paternalism, Child Support Enforcement and Fragile Families." In *The New Paternalism,* edited by Lawrence Mead. Washington, D.C.: Brookings Institution Press.

———. 2001. "The Responsible Fatherhood Field: Evolution and Goals." In *The Handbook of Father Involvement: Multidisciplinary Perspectives,* edited by Catherine Tamis-LeMonda and Natasha Cabrera. Mahwah, N.J.: Lawrence Erlbaum.

Nock, Steven L. 1998. *Marriage in Men's Lives.* New York: Oxford University Press.

Oliver, Melvin, and Thomas Shapiro. 1995. *Black Wealth/White Wealth: A New Perspective on Racial Inequality.* New York: Routledge.

Patterson, O. 1998. *Rituals of Blood: Consequences of Slavery in Two American Centuries.* Washington, D.C.: Civitas/CounterPoint.

Sorensen, E. 1995. "The Benefits of Increased Child Support Enforcement." Welfare Reform Briefs, no. 2. Washington, D.C.: Urban Institute.

Stack, Carol B. 1974. *All Our Kin: Strategies for Survival in a Black Community.* New York: Harper & Row.

Sullivan, Mercer. 1985. "Teen Fathers in the Inner City: An Exploratory Ethnographic Study." Report. New York: Ford Foundation.

———. 1993. "Young Fathers and Parenting in Two Inner-City Neighborhoods." In *Young Unwed Fathers: Changing Roles and Emerging Policies,* edited by R. I. Lerman and T. J. Ooms. Philadelphia: Temple University Press.

Tucker, M. B., and C. Mitchell-Kernan, eds. 1995. *The Decline in Marriage Among African Americans: Causes, Consequences, and Policy Implications.* New York: Russell Sage Foundation.

Waite, L. 2000. "Trends in Men's and Women's Well-Being in Marriage." In *The Ties That Bind: Perspectives on Marriage and Cohabitation,* edited by Linda Waite. New York: Walter de Gruyter.

Wilson, William Julius. 1996. *When Work Disappears: The World of the New Urban Poor.* New York: Alfred A. Knopf.

Zimmer, M. 1996. "Assortative Mating and Ethnicity in the Low Wage Population: An Examination of Spouses' Earnings." *Applied Economics Letters* 3(5): 311–15.

# Chapter 4

## THE MARRIAGE GAP: HOW AND WHY MARRIAGE CREATES WEALTH AND BOOSTS THE WELL-BEING OF ADULTS

### MAGGIE GALLAGHER

For understandable reasons, the marriage debate in this country has concentrated on the welfare of children. When mothers and fathers do not get and stay married, children are at increased risk for a whole host of problems and disorders: mental and physical illness, crime and delinquency, school failure, substance abuse, and teen pregnancy. Two decades of research has made clear that, as more than a hundred scholars and community leaders who signed a document titled "The Marriage Movement: A Statement of Principles" in the summer of 2000 put it, "Children do better, on average, when they are raised by their own two married parents" (Coalition for Marriage, Family, and Couples Education et al. 2000, 10). However, there is another case for marriage that is less well known. The evidence has been quietly building for decades that marriage is also a powerful creator and sustainer of adult well-being. Our book, *The Case for Marriage* (Waite and Gallagher 2000) reviews the vast scholarly literature on the relationship between marriage and adults' health, longevity, happiness, and financial success. The weight of evidence strongly points to marriage as a powerful generator and sustainer of adult human and social capital, arguably one as important as education in building the wealth and welfare of adults and communities.

Yet because marriage is increasingly being privatized in our society—conceptually reduced to an emotional relationship between two individuals, of little concern to anybody else except (possibly) their own children—the wealth that marriage produces is being very unequally distributed in our communities. In a culture in which marriage is viewed as just a private relationship, the vast benefits of marriage will be (and are) increasingly flowing to the already advantaged: those who are white, well-educated, higher-income, and whose parents got married and stayed married. As M. Belinda Tucker (2000) has noted, "African Americans marry later, are about twice as likely to divorce, and are less likely to marry ever, yet Blacks' views of the importance of marriage are similar to those held by members of other ethnic groups" (see also Bachrach, Hindin, and Thomson 2000). By age thirty, 80 percent of white women, but only 45 percent of black women, have married. Meanwhile, in 1995, 32 percent of the marriages of wives who are high school graduates had ended by the ten-year mark, compared to 18 percent of the marriages of college-educated wives (Abma et al. 1997, table 36).

Marriage is, to put it crudely, in itself a form of wealth. The unequal distribution of marriage in different communities feeds not only moral and spiritual distress but also pervasive inequalities in material health, wealth, and well-being among adults as well as children.

This is the case for marriage that has not yet been heard. It is of special interest for African American fathers and for those who care about building human and social capital in African American and other less-advantaged communities. For years social scientists toiling in their own fields have amassed powerful evidence of the benefits of marriage for adults. Labor economists researched the marriage premium for men; health researchers looked at the effect of marital status on illness; demographers calculated the longer life spans of the married; economists looked at wealth acquisition; research psychologists documented the better emotional and mental health of the married; and sexologists, at long last, created nationally representative studies of sexual behavior that also confirmed a powerful marital advantage. But few scholars have crossed disciplines to pull together this broad and deep body of evidence.

What do we know about how much marriage matters for adults? Let's begin with a topic of overwhelming interest in our aging society: long life and good health. Here the advantages of married life are truly astonishing. For example, Lee Lillard and Linda Waite (1995) looked at a large, nationally representative database to see how marriage, divorce, and remarriage affect men and women's mortality rates. How big a difference did marriage make? Put it this way: take twenty middle-aged men (forty-eight years old). Make them as alike as social scientists know how in terms of race, income, education, and health history, except that half are married and half are not. What are the chances these two men will make it to age sixty-five? The answer is that nine out of ten husbands, but just six out of ten single or divorced men will live that long. Three out of ten men (absent remarriage) would lose their lives when they lose their wives.

For women, marriage also had powerful protective effects, but not quite as large. Nine out of ten wives, but only eight out of ten single or divorced women who are alive at age forty-eight will live to be at least sixty-five years old (Lillard and Waite 1995, 1131–56). Lillard and Waite's research is confirmed by a large body of other health research which shows that married people live not only longer but also healthier lives. For example, being unmarried lowers a man's life expectancy by much more than being married with heart disease. In late middle age, married women are about 40 percent less likely than unmarried women to rate their health as only fair or poor. Married men and women are less likely than singles to suffer from long-term chronic illnesses or disabilities. As two demographers of mortality put it "[B]eing unmarried is one of the greatest risks that people voluntarily subject themselves to" (for a summary of this large body of research, see Waite and Gallagher 2000, 47–64; see also Cohen and Lee 1979, 707–22).

When it comes to emotional and mental health, the marriage gap is equally large. In popular discourse, divorce has increasingly been portrayed not as a sometimes necessary evil but as a positive social good, the gateway to happiness for adults and (therefore) to their children.

Although individuals' situations vary, the evidence should lead us to be deeply skeptical of the idea that divorce is a reliable path to happiness for adults. Overall, divorced people do not tell researchers that they are fabulously happy with life in general. In one national survey, just 18 percent of divorced persons said they were "very happy," compared to 40 percent of married persons. Married people are significantly happier than any other group, including singles and cohabitors, about a quarter of whom say they are "very happy."[1] These statistics may not capture the experience of the minority of divorced Americans who go on to make stable marriages that are happier than their first marriage. On the other hand, neither do they reflect, as some might suppose, only the immediate trauma of the divorce process. Research that follows individuals as they marry, divorce, and remarry (or not) have found that the negative effects of divorce on emotional well-being do not dissipate as time passes. Instead, the mental health of the divorced (absent remarriage) continues to deteriorate compared to that of married persons. Being divorced, not just getting divorced, seems to increase mental and emotional distress.

Nadine Marks and James Lambert (1998, 652–86), for example, looked at changes in the psychological health of men and women from the late eighties to the mid-nineties. They measured the mental health of individuals at the beginning of the study along a wide range of dimensions and then watched how mental health changed as individuals married, stayed married, divorced, stayed single, or stayed divorced over the five-year period. When people married, their mental health improved consistently and substantially. Meanwhile, as people divorced they suffered substantial deterioration in mental and emotional well-being, including increases in depression and declines in reported happiness. Those who divorced reported less of a sense of personal mastery, less positive relations with others, less purpose in life, and less self-acceptance than their married peers did. Divorce, they found, was especially damaging to women's mental health.

Nor is the greater happiness of the married simply an American phenomenon. One recent study by Steven Stack and J. Ross Eshleman (1998, 527–36) undertaken in seventeen developed nations found that "married persons have a significantly higher level of happiness than persons who are not married," even after they controlled for gender, age, education, children, church attendance, financial satisfaction, and self-reported health. Further, "[T]he strength of the association between being married and being happy is remarkably consistent across nations." Nor did having a live-in partner produce the same jump in well-being. Cohabitation did not increase financial satisfaction or perceived health at all, and cohabitors got only a small fraction of the happiness boost associated with marriage. Another large study, of 100,000 Norwegians, found that among both men and women, "[T]he married have the highest level of subjective well-being, followed by the widowed." Even long-divorced people who cohabited were not any happier than single people (Mastekaasa 1994, 665–92).

When it comes to making money and building wealth, marriage also plays a key role. Here again the social science evidence and the conventional wisdom are sharply at odds. Americans increasingly view marriage as a luxury consumption item. Sure, married people have more money, many argue, because it takes money to get married. There is more than a grain of truth in this popular cliché; certainly men who are chronically unemployed are unlikely to get and stay married. But this is not the whole story of the relationship between marriage and money. Married people earn more money and build more wealth than their single counterparts, because they are married. Marriage, in other words, is a productive, wealth-building institution, not an expensive consumer good.

When it comes to earnings and wealth, the marriage gap is substantial. As Linda Waite and I put it in *The Case for Marriage* (2000, 99), "The wage premium married men receive is one of the most well-documented phenomena in social science. Husbands earn at least 10 percent more than single men do and perhaps as high as 40 percent more." One economist estimates that each year of college adds about 7 percent to a man's income compared to a high school diploma (Schoeni 1995, 351–59). Thus, in the United States, though measures of the size of the marriage premium do vary, by at least some measures getting and keeping a wife may be as important to a man's career as getting a college education.

Why? When productivity can be measured directly, the reason for the marriage premium becomes clear: husbands earn more because they produce more than otherwise similar single men. Husbands are less likely to stalk out after a fight with a supervisor, to show up for work hung-over or sleep-deprived. They benefit, too, from their wives' help and counsel. One study looked at whether the wife's education affected her husband's earnings, after controlling for his own education. The answer? Yes, and powerfully. Husbands with college-educated wives earned almost 12 percent more than single men with comparable work and education histories. Husbands whose wives had high school diplomas earned just 4.3 percent more than comparable men, and men who married high school dropouts actually earned less than comparable single men. Wives' education remained a powerful predictor of husbands' earnings, regardless of whether or not they had children and regardless of whether or not the wives themselves were employed (Loh 1996, 566–89).

Married people also manage money better, acquiring more wealth and experiencing less financial stress than singles with similar incomes. At the same income levels, married couples are less likely to experience "economic hardship," defined as trouble paying basic bills. When a married man is tempted to go out and splurge on a fancy new computer, he may be free to do so, in the legal sense. But instead of being able to say it "ain't nobody's business if I do," he knows that at the very least he is going to have to go back home and explain to his wife exactly why that much of "the family" money really needed to be spent. The greater sense of financial responsibility married people have to each other produces better decisions over the long run than the absolute financial autonomy singles enjoy.

Marriage partners make more money and build more wealth for some of the same underlying reasons that business partnerships tend to be more productive than sole proprietorships. Married people have twice the talent pool, so they are twice as likely to find their home contains a good financial manager, for example. Married people can also "specialize" in a variety of ways that improve wealth income production, investment management, making inexpensive homemade meals instead of eating out, getting all the money owed out of insurance companies, finding the cheapest groceries, paying bills on time, or shopping for less expensive credit. Because married people do not have to do all of life's tasks, they have more time and energy and can become more skilled at the tasks they do assume.

Married people, working together as a team, produce more together than either would as a solo individual. When individuals have to do all of the tasks of business (or life) on their own, they do each of them less well than if they had a partner to double the talent and divide the burden.

Finally, the vows of marriage have an economic, as well as sentimental and psychological value. Married people promise to take care of each other in sickness and in health, in times of crisis (such as unemployment) as well as times of plenty. Married people provide these services to each other because they care about each other, and because social norms prescribe this kind of spousal caretaking. But a husband whose wife develops a disabling illness may drive her to work every day for another important reason: the money she makes is his money, too.

The insurance value alone of the marriage partnership substantially boosts wealth and well-being. A married couple form a small insurance pool against the uncertainties of life. Buying an insurance policy to cover the kind of support spouses routinely provide one another would be a very expensive proposition. Economists estimate that later in life, the insurance value of marriage alone in later years is equivalent to a 30 percent increase in wealth (Kotlikoff and Spivak 1981, 372–91).

Over time, the economic advantages of marriage translate into substantial wealth advantages. By late middle age the difference in individuals' wealth accumulation by marital status is profound. A RAND corporation study that looked at net worth of Americans in their fifties found that married couples (including remarriages) had a median net worth of $132,000, compared to about $34,000 for divorced, $47,000 for widowed, and $35,000 for never married individuals (Smith 1995, 7).

Faced with the research that shows a powerful relationship between marriage and adult wealth and well-being, many observers remain skeptical: How can a marriage license, a mere piece of paper, boost adults' earnings, wealth, happiness, and health? Surely the statistical advantage of the married is the product of statistical illusion: happy, healthy, and productive people are more likely to get and stay married. These selection effects, many believe, are what account for the apparent economic advantages of marriage. Certainly there are important selection effects in marriage, although they do not always function in the expected direction. Heavy drinkers, for example, are no less likely to marry than teetotalers, and men with health problems are actually more likely to marry than healthy men (Miller-Tuzauer, Leonard, and Windle 1991, 434–40; Lillard and Panis 1996, 313–27). Higher earnings lead to increases in marriage, as predicted, but also increases in cohabitation (although the effects of high relative income are stronger on entry into marriage than entry into cohabitation) (Clarkberg 1999, 945–68; see also table 2).

But there are strong reasons to doubt that such selection effects can explain away the marriage gap in adult wealth and well-being. For one thing, researchers who attempt to control for the confounding affects of race and family background continue to find powerful benefits from marriage in terms of health, emotional and physical well-being, longevity, earnings, and wealth acquisition. A smaller body of research, using longitudinal data, allows us to measure factors such as alcohol and substance use, indicators of mental distress and well-being prior to marriage (or to divorce), and thus to track how changes in marital status change individuals' behavior. By and large, these sorts of studies confirm that marriage is not just a ceremonial act; it is a powerful social institution that changes the way two people think about each other, their future, and their relationship with the wider society.

Moreover, the economic mechanisms by which marriage boosts well-being are increasingly well understood and hard to ignore: two incomes, significant economies of scale, twice the talent pool, the capacity to "specialize" and thereby boost production in both market-

and nonmarket production, the insurance value of a mate. While people in complex market economies no longer typically conceptualize marriage as an economic institution, both economic theory and empirical observations strongly suggest that marriage is in fact a wealth-producing organization.

Cohabitors could in theory reap a portion of the marriage benefit. They have two incomes, one rent, double the potential talent pool. But research suggests that cohabitors gain only a small part of the marriage benefit. The longer a couple stays married, the more wealth they build, but length of cohabitation has no association with wealth acquisition (Hao 1996, 269–92).

How can this be? Long-term cohabitors, it turns out, are not "just like" married couples. They are couples in which at least one of the partners has declined to marry. This does not seem to be a random act of lethargy, but a reflection of deliberate choice: one or both partners do not want the heavier responsibilities for the other person, including the burden of presumed permanence, that marriage represents. Cohabitors do not know how long they will be together; they are far less likely to view their assets as truly jointly shared; they accept less responsibility for their partners' economic and emotional support. Each is freer of responsibility for the long-term well-being of the other. The result, ironically, is that they do not reap the deeper benefits that come from a permanent union of bed and bank account. Because cohabitors are not publicly responsible for each other financially, they have less incentive to behave responsibly when it comes to money matters—to resist spending splurges, for example. Because they do not know what the future holds, cohabitors find it harder to plan together for it. They are less likely to "specialize" in ways that make them interdependent, and understandably so: it is dangerous to become dependent on a relationship that could end, if not any day, then any year.

By increasing couples' confidence that the relationship will last, marriage encourages specialization, and long-range planning. By prescribing shared norms for how married couples "ought" to behave, marriage changes the behavior of adult men and women in ways that make both men and women better off financially, physically, and emotionally.

So far we have been looking at research on the consequences of marriage for all couples. How does research suggest that the marriage gap affects African Americans? Many people have the impression

that the benefits of marriage for African Americans, while still substantial, are smaller than for whites. More research on this is needed,
but the available evidence suggests a more mixed picture. On some
measures, such as the health advantages for children, African
Americans do not reap the same benefits as Euro-Americans. Black
children from married homes are healthier than those from unmarried
ones, but the "health gap" is smaller—in part perhaps because far
fewer black children in married homes are in "intact" marriages.
Thirty-eight percent of black married mothers rate their child's health
as "excellent," compared to less than 31 percent of black single mothers. Black babies born out of wedlock are 40 percent more likely to die
before they celebrate their first birthday than black babies born to
married women. By contrast, 58 percent of white mothers say their
child's health is "excellent," compared to just 46 percent of white single mothers. And white babies born to unmarried moms are 70 percent more likely to die (Angel and Worobey 1988, 38–52). On the other
hand, when it comes to adult health, the marriage gap (as we shall see)
appears larger for African Americans than for whites (Pienta, Hayward, and Jenkins 2000, 559ff). And African American wives get a big-
ger marriage premium and pay less of a motherhood penalty in terms
of earnings than white wives. In one recent study childless white
wives received a 4 percent marriage premium, while childless black
wives earned 10 percent more than otherwise similar unmarried
women (Waite 1995, 483–507; Waldfogel 1997, 209–17). Determining
the relative benefits of marriage for African Americans compared
to other ethnic groups is complex and is a subject on which more
research, and a more comprehensive review of the research, is needed.

What we do know about the marriage gap for African American
children as well as adults is sobering. As children, of course, African
Americans are far more likely than whites to grow up in single-parent
homes and to be poor. Almost 70 percent of black children experience
a poverty spell by the age of seventeen, compared to about a quarter
of white children. African American children are not only more likely
to be poor, they are also far more likely to experience "dire" poverty:
household income only half of the poverty level. Just over 50 percent
of black children will experience dire poverty by age seventeen, compared to 12 percent of white children.

But the marriage gap in children's poverty is even greater than the
race gap: 81 percent of children who live in never-married households
fall into poverty by age seventeen, compared to 22 percent of children

in married households; 52 percent of children in unmarried households experience dire poverty in at least one year, compared to 10 percent of children in married households. The marriage gap in child poverty is also large compared to the education gap: 37 percent of children in families whose head has less than a high school education dip into dire poverty compared to 12 percent of children in families headed by an individual with at least a high school diploma.

Although African American children experience higher risk of poverty regardless of their parents' marital status, the marriage gap is also evident: 32 percent of black children living in a home whose head has at least a high school diploma and who also is married will have experienced at least one spell of poverty, compared to 85 percent living in a home whose head has a high school diploma but is unmarried (Rank and Hirschl 1999, 1058–67).

Less well known is how the negative effects of this "low-marriage regime" continue on into adulthood. As adults, African Americans marry later, are less likely to marry at all, and divorce more often than other Americans. Socioeconomic factors explain some of the marriage gap between African Americans and whites, but low-income African American men still "have nonmarital fathering rates two to three times greater than other low-income racial and ethnic groups" (Coley and Chase-Landsdale 1999, 416–35, 417). Disadvantaged as children, African Americans are much more likely grow up to be additionally disadvantaged as adults who do without the enormous social, financial, mental, and physical health benefits of stable marriage.

Most of the wider body of research on the benefits of marriage generally controls for race, so differences between races in their rate of entry into and out of marriage cannot explain away the benefits of marriage. When it comes to wealth accumulation, which some scholars argue is a better measure of economic well-being than income (see, for example, Oliver and Shapiro 1995), the marriage gap is even deeper for blacks than whites, although African Americans have much lower levels of wealth even after controlling for marital status.

Between the ages of fifty-one and sixty, married black couples have a median net worth of $59,000, compared to just $13,000 for divorced African Americans, and $200 for those who never married. "[M]arital disparities are much larger among blacks and Hispanics," notes the researcher (Smith 1995, 8). In late middle age, African Americans are less likely to be currently married: just 43 percent of blacks in their fifties were currently married, compared to 71 percent of whites.

African Americans were also more than twice as likely never to have married than whites, and also almost twice as likely to be currently divorced or separated than whites.

A similar large marriage gap in the health status of African Americans is becoming evident. When it comes to health, both a good in itself and a deep influence on wealth acquisition, a recent analysis of the Health and Retirement Study (Pienta et al. 2000), which looked at a nationally representative sample of 9,333 Americans between the ages of fifty-one and sixty-one in 1992, found that although "the benefits of marriage are conferred across all of the racial/ethnic groups . . . [t]he health benefits of marriage appear somewhat stronger among African Americans and Latinos than Whites with regard to fatal chronic conditions, with divorce having especially negative consequences for Latinos. Marriage confers even greater health benefits for African Americans and Latinos than Whites with regard to the nonfatal conditions, functioning problems, and disability" (Pienta et al. 2000, 571; see also table 3). In this study, people were defined as "disabled" if they said they had a physical limitation or illness that interfered with their ability to do either paid work or work around the home. Twenty-three percent of married African Americans in this age group have some disability, compared to 33 percent of cohabitors, 35 percent of the divorced, 40 percent of the widowed, and 39 percent of those who never married (Pienta et al. 2000, 559–86, 571, 574–75).[2] The researchers conclude that although selection effects may explain part of the greater returns on marriage for African American health, "We suspect that both strong selection processes and strong marital context effects are at work in providing married African Americans and Latinos better health than their unmarried counterparts" (Pienta et al. 2000, 582). In sum, the best evidence suggest that marriage is an important generator of economic and social wealth for Americans, families, and both white and black communities.

## NOTES

1. Tabulations by Linda J. Waite from the General Social Survey, 1990 to 1996 waves (Waite and Gallagher 2000, 67).

2. All these differences were statistically significant, except for the cohabitors, whose very small sample size in this age group (n = 68) relative to the married couples (n = 848) made meeting tests of significance difficult. See Waite and Gallagher (2000).

## REFERENCES

Abma, J., C., A. Chandra, W.D. Moser, L. Peterson, and L. Piccinino. 1997. "Fertility, Family Planning, and Women's Health: New Data from the 1995 National Survey of Family Growth." *Vital Health Statistics* 23(19): 1–114.

Angel, Ronald, and Jacqueline Low Worobey. 1988. "Single Motherhood and Children's Health." *Journal of Health and Social Behavior* 29(1): 38–52.

Bachrach, Christine, Michelle J. Hindin, and Elizabeth Thomson. 2000. "The Changing Shape of the Ties That Bind." In *The Ties That Bind: Perspectives on Marriage and Cohabitation,* edited by Linda J. Waite. New York: Aldine de Gruyter.

Clarkberg, Marin. 1999. "The Price of Partnering: The Role of Economic Well-Being in Young Adults' First Union Experiences." Social Forces 77(3): 945–68.

Coalition for Marriage, Family, and Couples Education and the Institute for American Values, and the Religion, Culture, and Family Project, University of Chicago. 2000. *The Marriage Movement: A Statement of Principles.* New York: Institute for American Values. Also available at: *www.marriagemovement.org.*

Cohen, Bernard L., and I-Sing Lee. 1979. "A Catalog of Risks." *Health Physics* 36 (June): 707–22.

Coley, Rebekah Levine, and P. Lindsay Chase-Lansdale. 1999. "Stability and Change in Paternal Involvement Among Urban African Fathers." *Journal of Family Psychology* 12(3): 416–35.

Hao, Lingxin. 1996. "Family Structure, Private Transfers, and the Economic Well-Being of Families with Children." *Social Forces* 75(1): 269–92.

Kotlikoff, Laurence J., and Avia Spivak. 1981. "The Family as an Incomplete Annuities Market." *Journal of Political Economy* 89(2): 372–91.

Lillard, Lee A., and Constantijn Panis. 1996. "Marital Status and Mortality: The Role of Health." *Demography* 33(3): 313–27.

Lillard, Lee A., and Linda J. Waite. 1995. "'Til Death Do Us Part': Marital Disruption and Mortality." *American Journal of Sociology* 100(5): 1131–56.

Loh, Eng Seng. 1996. "Productivity Differences and the Marriage Wage Premium for White Males." *Journal of Human Resources* 31(3): 566–89.

Marks, Nadine F., and James David Lambert. 1998. "Marital Status Continuity and Change Among Young and Midlife Adults: Longitudinal Effects on Psychological Well-Being." *Journal of Family Issues* 19(6): 652–86.

Mastekaasa, Arne. 1994. "The Subjective Well-Being of the Previously Married: The Importance of Unmarried Cohabitation and Time Since Widowhood or Divorce." *Social Forces* 73(2): 665–92.

Miller-Tuzauer, Carol, Kenneth E. Leonard, and Michael Windle. 1991. "Marriage and Alcohol Use: A Longitudinal Study of 'Maturing Out.' " *Journal of Studies on Alcohol* 52(5): 434–40.

Nock, Steven. 1998. "The Consequences of Premarital Fatherhood." *American Sociological Review* 63 (April): 250–63.

Oliver, Melvin L., and Thomas M. Shapiro. 1995. *Black Wealth, White Wealth: A New Perspective on Racial Inequality.* New York: Routledge.

Pienta, Amy Mehraban, M.D. Hayward, and K. R. Jenkins. 2000. "Health Consequences of Marriage for Retirement Years." *Journal of Family Issues* 21(5): 559–86.

Rank, Mark R., and Thomas A. Hirschl. 1999. "The Economic Risk of Childhood in America: Estimating the Probability of Poverty Across the Formative Years." *Journal of Marriage and the Family* 61 (November): 1058–67.

Schoeni, Robert F. 1995. "Marital Status and Earnings in Developed Countries." *Journal of Popular Economics* 8(4): 351–59.

Smith, James P. 1995. "Marriage, Assets, and Savings." Labor and Population Working Paper Series, publication 95-08. New York: Rand Corporation.

Stack, Steven, and J. Ross Eshleman. 1998. "Marital Status and Happiness: A 17-Nation Study." *Journal of Marriage and the Family* 60 (May): 527–36.

Tucker, M. Belinda. 2000. "Marital Values and Expectations in Context: Results from a 21-City Survey." In *The Ties That Bind: Perspectives on Marriage and Cohabitation,* edited by Linda J. Waite. New York: Aldine de Gruyter.

Waldfogel, Jane. 1997. "The Effect of Children on Women's Wages." *American Sociological Review* 62 (April): 209–17.

Waite, Linda J. 1995. "Does Marriage Matter?" *Demography* 32(4): 483–507.

Waite, Linda J., and Maggie Gallagher. 2000. *The Case for Marriage: Why Married People Are Happier, Healthier, and Better Off Financially.* New York: Doubleday.

# Chapter 5

## THE EFFECTS OF CRIME AND IMPRISONMENT ON FAMILY FORMATION

### OBIE CLAYTON AND JOAN MOORE

Marriage and marriage rates are affected by many social, economic, and demographic variables. Demographers place a great deal of emphasis on sex ratios and look for imbalances. Sociologists and economists argue that marriage is more than a mathematical model and is affected by employment, education, earnings, uncertain job prospects, military service, imprisonment, and other related factors (Farley 1991; Tucker and Taylor 1989; Glick 1976). However, all social scientists will agree that some individuals are more marriageable than others and certain variables have more explanatory power than others. In our opinion, although researchers have pointed out with a high degree of accuracy the number of minority men behind bars or on parole or probation, incarceration has not yet been given nearly enough attention in the literature as a key factor in the decline in marriage rates for African Americans.

This chapter concentrates on the effects of prison on family formation and community stability. The higher the rate of imprisonment, the greater the number of socially and economically handicapped ex-inmates there are who strain existing family networks and are handicapped in forming new ones. This choice of incarceration as a method of social control ignores the impact of imprisonment, parole, and probation supervision: incarceration, even short-term, versus alternatives to incarceration pose different issues for communities.

### AFRICAN AMERICAN FAMILY DISINTEGRATION AND IMPRISONMENT

Our studies suggest that one of the biggest casualties of this incarceration of African American men has been the nuclear family. In most cultures, the family represents the foundation that nourishes achievement, provides support, enhances self-esteem, shapes our ideals and goals, and tempers our behavior. Marriage represents the foundation of the family. Without marriage, the concept of family changes. The once-cherished two-parent African American family is vanishing. In 1960, 73 percent of black families were married couples, whereas in 1993, 46 percent of black families were of this type, representing a decline of 27 percent (U.S. Bureau of the Census 1992). The failure of black men and women to marry is understood to be a leading factor in the crisis affecting today's African American family (Billingsley 1990). We focus here on how incarceration as the societal response to antisocial behavior has become increasingly self-destructive, generating family disintegration, which leads to more criminal activity.

## THE PRISONIZATION OF BLACK AMERICA

During the past three decades, the number of Americans behind bars has increased tremendously, at a rate exceeding 6 percent per year. In terms of aggregate numbers, approximately 2 million Americans (461 per 100,000) are currently in prison or jail (Russell Sage Foundation 2003). The United States now has the highest recorded incarceration rate of any nation in the world, having surpassed South Africa and the Soviet Union. However, such statistics paint only a partial picture of incarceration in the United States. Historically, certain ethnic and demographic subgroups, such as African Americans and males, have been incarcerated at higher rates than either whites or women. The recent increases in incarceration rates have been disproportionately absorbed by African American men. To make the preceding point more salient, look at what has occurred between 1978 and 1997: during this twenty-year period the total U.S. adult prison population more than quadrupled, from 246,581 to 1,195,498. Of this increase of 948,917 persons, 426,397, or 45 percent, were African American. These figures do not include another 800,000 African American men who were either in local jails, on probation, or on parole in 1997 (Russell Sage Foundation 2003).

A 1997 study commissioned by the Urban Institute, entitled "Did Getting Tough on Crime Pay?" (Sabol and Lynch 1997), reports that six times more African Americans are incarcerated than their white counterparts. If we were to disaggregate the figures we would find that one-third of African American men between the ages of twenty and twenty-nine are either in prison or jail. Applying life-table analyses to incarceration rates we discover that for blacks in the United States resident population, it is likely that 16.2 percent, regardless of their sex, will be admitted to prison during their lives; they are nearly twice as likely as Hispanics (9.4 percent) and six times more likely than whites (2.5 percent) to be imprisoned (Bonczar and Beck 1997). Many legal and extralegal factors have been cited for the high incarceration rates of African Americans. Racial profiling, mandatory minimum sentences, and especially the disparities in drug laws have had a dramatic effect on the incarceration rates of young males, especially in urban inner-city neighborhoods.

Michael Tonry (1995, 151) asserts that the effects of these "recent punishment policies [has been] to destabilize inner-city communities." At low levels of incarceration what happens to felons, both in prison and when they are released, is largely an individual and family matter. Whatever happens to them is not terribly important to their communities; there aren't enough of them to matter. However, at high levels of incarceration, what happens to them is important to their communities. Anti-drug laws have resulted in a dramatic increase in the imprisonment rates in inner-city communities. There are more men and women from such communities in prison, more ex-offenders on their streets—not just isolated individuals—and more of their families are affected. In turn, people who have not been directly involved with the criminal justice system begin to be affected. Existing strains within the community are exacerbated.

## THE EFFECTS OF ILLEGAL DRUGS ON INCARCERATION RATES

The intent of this chapter is not to argue that violent or sociopathic offenders should not be locked up, but rather, to argue that too many African Americans are being taken out of their families and communities for nonviolent and other property crimes, weakening both family and community. Marc Mauer (1991), assistant director of the Sentencing Project, has stated, "[T]he impact of the war on drugs has been responsible for much of the increase in the prison population, with 46 percent of new court commitments since 1980 being due to drug offenses." Highlighting this point, *USA Today*, in a special edition on drugs and race, presented the startling statistic that even though African Americans constitute less than 16 percent of cocaine users, they accounted for approximately 44 percent of all drug arrests ("Special Report: Drugs and Race," December 30, 1989). This study was supported by research from the National Institute of Drug Abuse that estimated that 80 percent of all cocaine abusers in the United States are white and 14 percent black.

The irony of the war against drugs is that more young men are being apprehended and convicted but drug use is increasing. The criminal justice system has begun to admit that it alone cannot stop illegal drug use and no longer wants to be burdened with the responsibility of doing so (Sabol and Lynch 1997). Conservative estimates on the costs associated with this war on drugs are put at $100 billion for the period 1970 to 1996. Even more startling than the costs is how these funds have been allocated—for example, only 3 percent of these monies were spent on rehabilitation and education programs. These statistics illustrate the need for us to reevaluate our national drug policies. We as a nation must realize that 90 percent of prisoners reenter society and many of them lack either education or job skills, forcing many to commit further crimes in an effort to survive. The Russell Sage Foundation "Future of Work" (2003) working group on mass incarceration supports the preceding assertion and shows that for low-skilled men, a 10 percent decrease in real wages in the formal labor market results in a 10 to 20 percent increase in criminal activity. A lack of formal education and unemployment are highly correlated with criminal offending.

The increased rate of imprisonment in the past three decades has coincided with a number of deleterious changes in the inner city. In particular, economic restructuring has ravaged job opportunities for poorly educated men and women of color. Many are unemployed or have dropped out of the labor market altogether. Bruce Western and Becky Pettit (2000) argue that incarceration severely limits the employment opportunities of African American men. Western further states that the nation's unemployment figures fail to take the incarcerated population into account when discussing unemployment in the labor market. Western shows that when the incarcerated population is counted as part of the labor pool, the employment figures for young black males steadily declined between 1982 and 1996. The lack of opportunity in the labor market has forced many young African American males into an informal economy that features illicit as well as legal jobs.

One important new aspect of inner-city communities is that criminalized activities, particularly drug marketing, have become a significant segment of their economy (Hagedorn 1994, 264–94). In this economic climate, the risk of imprisonment is almost "a form of business license tax" (Bullock 1973, 113). At the same time, many black communities have been hard hit by drug abuse and the violence that is often associated with drug dealing. Increased imprisonment of local dealers has rarely helped.

## AFRICAN AMERICAN WOMEN AND THE CRIMINAL JUSTICE SYSTEM

Confounding the problem is that drug-related crimes are not the sole domain of males. Since crack cocaine hit the street in the 1980s, women have been increasingly represented among users and dealers. What has gone virtually unnoticed in the literature is that the incarceration rate for African American females has increased at a rate higher than for black males since the mid-1980s. According to 1996 Uniform Crime Report data, the incarceration rate for African American women was 456 per 100,000. White and Latina women experienced an incarceration rate of 68 per 100,000 (Bureau of Justice Statistics 1996). The female incarceration rate has been increasing at a dramatic pace; between 1986 and 1995 the number of women in prison increased by 250 percent. This is ironic because the female crime rate increased by only 38 percent during this time period. The prevailing explanation for this high imprisonment rate is that judges are giving harsher sentences regardless of gender (Currie 1998). About 55 percent of admissions to prisons are for crimes that used to carry probation as a penalty (Bureau of Justice Statistics 1999). Convictions related to violent crime are more prevalent among imprisoned women, as they are less likely than men to be sent to prison for nonviolent offenses. However, African American women appear to be receiving the brunt of the "get tough" policy. For example, with all things being equal, if a pregnant black woman is convicted of a drug offense, she is ten times more likely than a white woman to spend time in prison.

The increase in the number of African American women in prison has deleterious effects on their families. Imprisoned women who give birth are separated from their children usually within a few days after the birth, thus severely weakening the mother-child bond. Moreover, a significant number of these women have young children at home, and it is the children who suffer most from such separations.

The increasing number of female inmates poses different problems for inner-city communities than those posed by men. As previously stated, contemporary drug laws have sent large numbers of women to prison. Most of them are mothers and, unlike male inmates, most were the primary care givers prior to imprisonment (Krisberg 1995; Schaenman 1995). Ann Stanton (1980), in one of the few studies of the families of jailed mothers (who were predominantly Chicanas and African Americans), paints a picture of severe disruption during the mother's jail term. In addition, the usual problems faced by an inmate upon release—finding money, a job, and a place to live—are exacerbated for women with children (Chesney-Lind 1998). A recurring theme is: who will take care of the children? Children of inmate mothers suffer severe displacement and this affects them throughout their lives.

In recent years many more grandmothers have been recruited as caregivers for the children of imprisoned parents. Grandparent caregivers face special problems, both personal and in dealing with bureaucratic regulations (Minkler and Roe 1993). Though grand-parental foster care is traditional in African American and Latino communities, an element of coercion has been added to what is historically an economic and social expedient. What happens when grandparents cannot care for the children of prisoners may become increasingly important in the future.

A growing body of literature suggests that children who have a parent in prison are much more likely than those who don't to become involved with drugs, experience difficulty in school, engage in delinquent acts, and suffer from other emotional problems (Butterfield 1999). These problems are dramatically increased when the incarcerated parent is the mother (Karen 1994). In addition to the social and behavioral problems experienced by children who have an incarcerated parent, communities also suffer.

## GROWING UP IN A CRIMINAL ENVIRONMENT: JUVENILES AND CRIME

The statistics clearly indicate that the youth of our country are committing a disproportionate amount of the crime and especially the violent crime that is committed. African American youth in this regard are caught up in a larger national trend across race. James Allen Fox (1996) points out: "From 1985 to 1994, the rate of murder committed by teens, ages 14–17, increased 172 percent. The rate of killing rose sharply for both black and white male teenagers, but not for females." Between 1978 and 1993 the homicide rate for juveniles rose about 177 percent, whereas while the adult rate for this same period dropped 7 percent (Blumstein 1995). During the period 1985 to 1994 the juvenile crime rate rose by 79 percent for the crimes of aggravated assault, rape, and robbery. In 1985, person offenses committed by juveniles accounted for only 16 percent of the caseload. In 1994 juvenile courts handled 336,100 person offenses, which made up 22 percent of the docket. An examination of violent crimes committed by juveniles between 1983 and 1993 reveals that they committed 128,000 crimes against the person or 19 percent of all violent crime (Abruzzese 1997). Overall, arrests for violent crimes rose 46 percent for teenagers but only 12 percent for adults. Further, homicide and other violent acts against persons have been increasing most rapidly among younger segments of the youthful population: between 1989 and 1994, the arrest rate for youth (children) aged fourteen to seventeen has overtaken that of young adults aged eighteen to twenty-four (Fox 1996).

The juvenile homicide figures are especially unnerving. The following findings from a study conducted by James Allen Fox (1996) indicate that violent crime among our youth is rampant:

- Although constituting just over 1 percent of the population, black males fourteen to twenty-four years of age now constitute 17 percent of the victims of homicide and over 30 percent of the perpetrators.

- Guns, and especially handguns, have played a major role in the surge of juvenile murder. Since 1984, the number of juveniles killing with a gun has quadrupled while the number killing with all other weapons combined has remained virtually constant.

- The largest increase in juvenile homicide involves offenders who are friends and acquaintances of their victims.

- By the year 2005, the number of teens aged fourteen to seventeen will increase by 20 percent, with a larger increase, 26 percent, among blacks in this age group.

- Even if the per-capita rate of teen homicide remains the same, the number of individuals in the 14–17-year-old age group who will commit murder should increase to nearly 5,000 annually because of changing demographics. And if offending rates continue to rise because of worsening conditions for our nation's youth, the number of teen killings could increase even more.

The juvenile crime rate is extremely disturbing because it increases the likelihood that these youths will engage in subsequent adult criminality, thus leading to a life characterized by lower levels of education, marginal jobs, and lower lifetime earnings. All of these factors affect the structure of the family.

Why are youths turning to crime? The correctional literature suggests that the shock effect of prison deters individuals from becoming recidivists. Despite such assertions, it has been found that the earlier a person is exposed to the prison environment, "the more they get used to it, and prison loses its stigma" (Butterfield 1999; Clear 2001). If this is true then we have a serious problem in this country: note that approximately 1.96 million children have a parent or immediate relative in prison on a given day, and another 1 million having a parent or relative who has served time in the past (Butterfield 1999). As Larry Sherman states, "[I]f you increase the number of people arrested and sent to prison, you may actually be creating another problem. There is a multiplier effect" (Sherman et al. 1997).

The number and proportion of African Americans who are in prison is an extremely grave problem in American society. Many scholars have pointed out that there are more African American men under correctional supervision than there are in colleges and universities (Snell 1995; Mauer and Chesney-Lind 2002). Given these startling statistics, it is highly unlikely that one would be able to find an inner-city child who does not know someone who either is in prison now or has been. As Larry Sherman suggests, this phenomenon has serious implications for the youths in these communities, who oftentimes view doing time as a rite of passage. M. B. Spencer and C. Markstrom-Adams (1990) suggest that these negative role models prevent many youths from actively planning and organizing their lives according to accepted standards. Further, criminal involvement and other forms of aberrant behavior bind this population together, which goes a long way toward ensuring that they will not be involved in mainstream America (Wilson 1987).

The explanations offered by Spencer and Markstrom-Adams (1990) borrow heavily from the work of Edwin Sutherland (1973), who advanced the theory of differential association as the major cause of crime. For Sutherland, criminal behavior is learned in a social environment that rewards, directly or indirectly, criminal behavior. Psychologists and social psychologists such as Jerome Kagan, and Howard A. Moss (1962), and Jean Piaget (1952, 1954, 1976) also argue that children learn by imitating, identifying with, and internalizing the actions of their parents or guardians. The children of inmates have seen their parents arrested, they have visited prisons, and quite often they have seen them engage in criminal activities. The people in their neighborhoods are very similar to their parents and in time they identify with the criminal way of life. They view the economics of crime such as drug dealing and fencing as a good way of life and find it much better than working at a minimum-wage job.

These youths often have a difficult time entering the labor force to begin with in the absence of family, friends, and neighbors who are in a position to hire them or serve as intermediaries. The criminal record that many carry with them places them at a further distinct disadvantage in the labor market, as they become what Wilson (1987) called the "left behinds." Western found that incarceration functioned as a key life event, one that triggered a cumulative spiral of disadvantage, lowering wages and wage growth over a man's life span. Incarceration was estimated to reduce earnings by 10 to 20 percent, and the rate of wage growth was reduced by 30 percent (Western 2001). Understanding the factors responsible for the worsening labor-market position of African Americans is a prerequisite to developing effective policies and training programs designed to ameliorate their plight. Prison, for youthful offenders, is not an effective solution to the problems confronting the nation. As we will attempt to illustrate, incarceration for this population may actually increase criminal offending.

## PRISONIZATION AND THE STRENGTHENING OF GANG AND NEIGHBORHOOD PEER GROUPS

The term "prisonization" refers to the "negative effects of institutionalization on prisoners' commitment to prosocial norms, values, and beliefs" (Bowker 1977)—in other words, what the inmate carries with him when he leaves the physical prison. These subcultural effects are more serious for younger inmates and are exacerbated by longer sentences. And in recent years, sentences have been lengthening (Tonry 1995).

For younger inmates, prison serves to strengthen and reinforce neighborhood criminal ties. One researcher remarked that concentrated neighborhood-based law-enforcement strategies such as New York's Tactical Narcotics Teams have turned Rikers Island, a New York City jail, "into a [neighborhood] block party!" (Curtis et al. 1994). All of the drug dealers in the neighborhood, those who are gang members and those who aren't, are swept into jail at the same time. Prisons and jails are ideal institutions for strengthening peer-group relationships that have later repercussions on the streets.

Yet an absence of family and neighborhood ties early in life is also problematical. Not all inmates come to prison with strong ties to the outside world. State-raised youths whose adolescent years have involved frequent probation supervision and trips to juvenile detention facilities and whose young-adult years have been spent in and out of prison have only the most fragile ties to family and friends in the community. These youths are the most fully prisonized. In California, they have been held responsible for the development of the more violent prison gangs, such as the Mexican Mafia and Nuestra Familia (Moore et al. 1978). Although these gangs developed in prison, they were exported to the streets and by now are established criminal organizations. In several states, law enforcement and media allege that criminal street gangs are controlled by prison inmates. Increased imprisonment of women enlarges the number of young men who have been raised in state-run institutions and lowers the age of first imprisonment.

The problem is not simply the number of ex-offenders on the streets but the way their experience comes to pervade the social networks in which they participate—the way the widely shared life experience of brutalization that pervades prisons impacts the culture of released inmates involved in street networks. Prisons are single sex, very racist, and often very violent. Researchers and practitioners within the criminal justice system speculate that the increased violence in street networks may result from the export of violent prison interpersonal styles. There is some evidence that ex-inmates hang around with younger men, who are impressed by these "veteranos." These are "dinosaurs, roaming the streets long after their time is gone," according to one former gang member (Moore 1991, 123). Often younger members of these street groups are the only people from whom ex-inmates can command deference.

Such street networks may be relatively impervious to sanctions, formal or informal. Their members become inured to criminal justice sanctions, and their friends do not stigmatize them if they do wind up in prison. The prisoner subculture is intensely hostile to established authority, and these attitudes, too, are exported to the streets. In the early 1980s, surveys attempting to measure criminal activity were conducted among inner-city African American youths in several cities. Among those who admitted committing a crime, approximately three-quarters felt that they faced very little chance of going to prison, and even if they did, the vast majority—92 percent—felt that they would not lose friends (Viscusi 1986, but see also Broadsky 1975).

For many families, the criminal justice system, including prison, is a painfully familiar bureaucracy bordering on the routine. For others, there may be an omnipresent threat of imprisonment, since many inner-city families that are basically law-abiding are also involved in petty hustling (Valentine 1978). The pervasiveness of prison in these communities means that parents and spouses of inmates can expect to receive support from extended kin, neighbors, members of their churches, and friends. Does this fact relate to the much-discussed—but also little-studied—issue of whether inner-city communities are more tolerant of deviance? The answer probably involves variation both in inner-city community composition and also in what is meant by deviance. Routinization of prison may result in inner-city youths' becoming "presocialized" to prison. Every additional inmate released to the community increases the chances that community youths will learn directly about prison and become yet more persuaded that prison lies in their own futures. For inner-city youths, anticipatory socialization to prison is exacerbated by the fact that images of prison life permeate the national youth culture well beyond ghettos and barrios (Krisberg 1995). Prison-style clothing, celebrity "gangsta rappers," and images of prison on MTV pervade middle-class white youth culture. For at-risk youth, this commodification of prison glamorizes the prison experience. What is trendy play for the children of the middle class is all too real for those in the inner city.

What really happens to them once they are incarcerated and released?

## POST-PRISON MARGINALIZATION AND RECIDIVISM

After reuniting with their families, getting work is the most pressing concern for men and women released from prison (Moore et al.

1978), but they are rarely successful (Petersilia 2000). There is almost no assistance provided to ensure that this extremely difficult transition is successful. Annually, over 500,000 parolees are leaving prison and resettling in mostly low-income, resource-strapped communities. In 1998, a mere 7,200 of the approximately 142,000 inmates released from prison in California had completed a reentry program prior to release (Petersilia 2000). In 1991, only 21 percent of California's parolees were working full-time (Irwin and Austin 1994). The prison experience is profoundly destructive of work habits. During most of their time in prison, inmates are idle, and most of the relatively rare prison work is characterized by a slowdown that represents resistance to authority (Correctional Association of New York 1984; Vigil 1989). Inmates rarely come out of prison with enhanced job skills, and they often acquire very dysfunctional work habits and attitudes. The ordinary strains typical of a civilian workplace are difficult for them. In general, the earlier in life the person experiences prison, the more dysfunctional the later work habits (Jeffery Fagan, personal communication, 1995).

A prison record presents an obstacle to finding a job, and so does the intense post-release parole surveillance, which often interferes with work. Parolees return to prison more often for technical violations than for new crimes (Irwin and Austin 1994). Immediate post-release difficulties in obtaining work lead many former prisoners to adopt an idle lifestyle and preprison peer and associations that go with it. They hang out, and their wives continue to bear the burden of supporting the family financially and emotionally (Fishman 1990). These lifestyles impede adaptation to work, even under the most supportive working conditions (Padfield and Williams 1973).

Already marginalized men and women become even more marginalized (Glasgow 1981). Ex-inmates' joblessness may have the most significant effect on their surroundings—their families and communities. Prison erodes inmates' sexual, social, and coping skills. In particular, the baggage from the prison experience erodes marriages, and newly released inmates have difficulty in reestablishing old relationships or forming new ones that extend beyond casual sex. Men often lack money, a car, and other resources necessary for dating. Once in a domestic setting, the former inmates may be prone to greater domestic violence. It is particularly difficult for women to form relationships after they have been in prison (Moore and Mata 1981). Increased rates of imprisonment mean there will be greater numbers of such economically and socially impaired men and women on the streets, leading to greater familial and community disruption.

For a significant fraction of ex-offenders, the obstacles to obtaining jobs and establishing stable families become insuperable. Anecdotal data from several field researchers supply substantial evidence of what John Irwin and James Austin (1994) call dereliction. After they exhaust family resources, many ex-offenders wind up on the streets, homeless. Rossi, in a 1989 study of homeless men, found that an average of 21.3 percent had served prison sentences. This figure is probably higher today.

## GENDER ROLE MODELING

A large body of literature on poor African American males argues that the street subculture plays a major role in their lives. Its importance is inversely proportional to the men's weakened job chances and, perhaps, to their vulnerability to arrest and imprisonment, although the latter is rarely mentioned (Anderson 1990; Majors and Billson 1992). Street subcultures are substantially influenced by the presence of ex-offenders, and by the expectation of many members of the subculture that they, too, will wind up doing time.

Among numerous significant aspects of street subcultures is one that is particularly relevant here: what Majors and Billson (1992, 8) call the "cool" male pose, a stance adopted by many inner-city men to cope with the threats to their self-respect that they often encounter. This façade of aloofness and control, according to the authors, "counters the . . . damaged pride [and] shattered confidence . . . that come from living on the edge of society." The cool pose is particularly well suited to the inmate role—the prison norm that one should "hold one's mud"—not show any emotion—and in this respect the pose transcends racial subcultures. The prison experience and the post-prison adaptations of inner-city men contribute to the all male orientation of the street culture and reinforce the cool pose—with all of its ramifications.

The cool pose also inhibits the formation of nurturant relationships, according to Majors and Billson (1992). Young black fathers who cannot find jobs experience severe strains. They lose power in relationships with their children and girlfriends and, as a result, depreciate the institution of marriage altogether (Laseter 1991). Their scorn for marriage is part of the cool pose.

## IMPACT ON MARRIAGE: DEPLETION AND PRISON
## RECORD APARTHEID

It has been argued that the mere fact of taking a community's men away to prison—the so-called "depletion effect," has strong negative consequences for family formation. Perhaps the most widely discussed impact of the depletion effect is that it contributes to the shortage of "marriageable males." Wilson (1987) framed this discussion by noting the sharp decline among African Americans in the ratio of men with jobs to every women of the same age. As the proportion of young black men who are imprisoned or on parole has grown to 20 to 29 percent and the numbers of young black women imprisoned increase rapidly, roughly one quarter of young African Americans are directly impacted in their efforts to form and maintain families. Rates of imprisonment for black men have been increasing more than 6 percent a year (Blumstein 1995, 1–16), and are projected to increase even more (Irwin and Austin 1994). Thus, however damaging the depletion effect is now, it may well become even worse in the future.

Benjamin Bowser (1995) argues that if one is concerned with the effect of the criminal justice system on marriageability, the depletion effect—the absence of men—is less important than the fact that having a prison or jail record lowers employment chances and thus lowers marriageability (Sampson and Laub 1995). This broadens the concern: instead of focusing only on those who are in prison, we must look at men living in the community who have criminal records of any sort and at the ways in which short-term incarceration affects work. Though data are not firm, conservative estimates suggest that as many as a quarter to a third of young African American males have records. Field studies of low-income communities leave no doubt that in some neighborhoods and in some networks there are even higher percentages (Benjamin Bowser, personal communication, 1995; Moore et al. 1978). Given what we know about multiplier effects of prisonization on the socialization of youth, the normative order of social life, and political efficacy, it is clear that the sector of African American families affected is much larger than the approximately 25 percent of potential heads-of-family who are in prison or are ex-offenders.

## WHERE DO WE GO FROM HERE?

We have tried to illustrate in this paper that incarceration has dramatically affected the African American family and community. Our central findings:

- Almost one in three potential African American family formations by people aged twenty to twenty-nine is severely impacted or destroyed by the prevention of marriageable status for the men through the criminal justice system—they are in prison or jail, on probation, or on parole.

- The imprisonment of African American men leads to low educational attainment and low earnings capacity, preventing their attainment of a lifestyle above the poverty line. This is directly related to the fact that more African American men are under the control of the prison system than are involved in higher education.

- The fastest-growing segment of the prison population is African American females. The stress on the African American family and community is rapidly becoming compounded by the removal of mothers, often the only subsistence providers, from their children.

The grim facts show how African Americans are overrepresented in our prison system. A sizable number of African Americans have simply given up hope and have removed themselves from the mainstream of society. Many of our African American youths have adopted a counterculture lifestyle that has made them unattractive to potential employers. These youths are truly America's disadvantaged, and often lack family or community support. The disadvantaged youths of today become tomorrow's unemployed, undereducated, stigmatized, and criminalized fathers within the struggling black community. We are at a point in our nation's history where we cannot simply lock them up and throw away the key.

---

I would like to thank my research assistant, Brandeis Malbrue, for her assistance, and the Vera Institute of Justice for allowing us to use portions of Dr. Moore's prior research. Also, I wish to thank Dr. Cynthia Hewitt for comments and suggestions for this chapter.

## REFERENCES

Abruzzese, George. 1997. *Juvenile Crime: Approaching the Millennium.* Accessed March 30, 2000, at: *www.juvenilejustice.com/millennium.html30.*

Anderson, Elijah. 1990. *Street Wise: Race, Class and Change in an Urban Community.* Chicago: University of Chicago Press.

Billingsley, Andrew. 1990. "Understanding Black Family Diversity." In *The State of Black America 1990,* edited by J. Dewart. New York: National Urban League.

Blumstein, Alfred. 1995. "Violence by Young People: Why the Deadly Nexus?" *National Institute of Justice Journal* (U.S. Department of Justice) 229(August): 1–20.

Bonczar, Thomas P., and Allen J. Beck. 1997. *Lifetime Likelihood of Going to State or Federal Prison.* Bureau of Justice Statistics bulletin no. NCJ 160092. Washington: U.S. Department of Justice.

Bowker, Lee H. 1977. *Prisoner Subcultures.* Lexington, Mass.: Lexington Books.

Bowser, Benjamin P. 1995. *Racism and Anti-Racism in World Perspective.* Thousand Oaks, Calif.: Sage Publications.

Broadsky, S. L. 1975. *Families and Friends of Men in Prison.* Lexington, Mass.: Lexington Books.

Bullock, Paul. 1973. *Aspiration vs. Opportunity.* Ann Arbor, Mich.: Institute of Industrial and Labor Relations.

Bureau of Justice Statistics. 1996. *Sourcebook of Criminal Justice Statistics.* Available at: *www.ojp.usdoj.gov/bjs.*

———. 1999. "Prisoners in 1998." Bureau of Justice Statistics Bulletin no. NCJ 175687. Washington: U.S. Department of Justice.

Butterfield, Fox. 1999. *All God's Children: The Bosket Family and the American Tradition of Violence.* New York: Avon Books.

Chesney-Lind, Meda. 1998. "Women in Prison: From Partial Justice to Vengeful Equity." *Corrections Today* 60: 66–73.

Clear, Todd R. 2001. "Has Academic Criminal Justice Come of Age?" *Justice Quarterly* 18(4): 709–26.

Clear, Todd R., and David R. Karp. 1999. *The Community Justice Ideal: Preventing Crime and Achieving Justice.* Boulder, Colo.: Westview Press.

Correctional Association of New York. 1984. "Doing Idle Time." Report. New York: Correctional Association of New York.

Currie, Dawn H. 1998. "Violent Men or Violent Women? Whose Definition Counts?" In *Issues in Intimate Violence,* edited by R. Kennedy Bergen. Thousand Oaks, Calif.: Sage Publications.

Curtis, Richard, Samuel R. Friedman, Alan Negaigus, Benny Jose, Marjorie Goldstein, and Gilbert Ildefonso. 1994. *Street-Level Drug Markets: Network Structure and HIV Risk.* New York: National Development and Research Institutes.

Farley, Reynolds. 1991. "Residential Segregation of Social and Economic Groups and Blacks: 1970–1980." In *The Urban Underclass,* edited by Christopher Jencks and Paul E. Peterson. Washington, D.C.: Brookings Institution Press.

Fishman, Laura T. 1990. *Women at the Wall.* Albany: State University of New York Press.

Fox, James Allen. 1996. *Methods in Quantitative Criminology.* New York: Academic Press.

Glasgow, Douglass. 1981. *The Black Underclass.* San Francisco: Jossey-Bass.

Glick, Paul C. 1976. "Updating the Life Cycle of the Family." *Journal of Marriage and the Family* 39(1): 5–13.

Hagedorn, John. 1994. "Neighborhood, Markets, and Gang Drug Organizations." *Journal of Research in Crime and Delinquency* 31(3): 264–94.

Irwin, John, and James Austin. 1994. *It's About Time: America's Imprisonment Binge.* Belmont, Calif.: Wadsworth.

Kagan, Jerome, and Howard A. Moss. 1962. *Birth to Majority: A Study in Psychological Development.* New Haven, Conn.: Yale University Press.

Karen, Richard. 1994. *Becoming Attached.* New York: Warner Books.

Krisberg, Barry. 1995. "The Unintended Consequences of Incarceration." Paper from a conference organized by the Vera Institute for Justice. Available at: *www.vera.org/publication_pdf/uci.pdf.*

Krisberg, Barry, and Michael A. Jones. 1994. "Images and Reality: Juvenile Crime, Youth Violence and Public Policy." *National Council on Crime and Delinquency.*

Laseter, Richard. 1991. "Black Men: Work and Family Life." Paper presented at Urban Poverty and Family Life Conference, University of Chicago (October 10–12).

Majors, Richard, and Janet Billson. 1992. *Cool Pose.* New York: Simon & Schuster.

Mauer, Marc. 1991. "The Problems of African-American Males and the Criminal Justice System." Paper presented to the Senate Committee on Banking, Housing, and Urban Affairs (March 19).

———. 1994. "Americans Behind Bars: The International Use of Incarceration." Washington, D.C.: The Sentencing Project.

Mauer, Marc, and Meda Chesney-Lind, eds. 2002. *Invisible Punishment: The Collateral Consequences of Mass Incarceration.* New York: New Press.

Minkler, Mevedah, and Kathleen Roe. 1993. *Grandmothers as Caregivers.* Newbury Park, Calif.: Sage Publications.

Moore, Joan, R. Garcia, C. Garcia, L. Cerda, and F. Valencia. 1978. *Homeboys: Gangs, Drugs, and Prison in the Barrios of Los Angeles.* Philadelphia: Temple University Press.

Moore, Joan, and A. Mata. 1981. *Women and Heroin in Chicano Communities.* Los Angeles: Chicano Pinto Research Project.

Moore, M. 1991. "Violence, Race, and the Police." Unpublished paper. Harvard University: Program in Criminal Justice Policy and Management, John F. Kennedy School of Government.

Padfield, Harland, and Roy Williams. 1973. *Stay Where You Are: A Study of Unemployables in Industry.* Philadelphia: J.P. Lippincott.

Petersilia, Joan. 2000. "Challenges of Prisoner Reentry and Parole in California." California Policy Research Brief series vol. 12, no. 4. Available at: *www.ucop.edu/cprc/publist.html#criminal.*

Piaget, Jean. 1952. *Judgment and Reasoning in the Child.* New York: Humanities Press.

———. 1954. *The Construction of Reality in the Child.* New York: Basic Books.

———. 1976. *The Grasp of Consciousness: Action and Concept in the Young Child.* Cambridge, Mass.: Harvard University Press.

Rossi, Peter. 1989. *Down and Out in America: The Origins of Homelessness.* Chicago: University of Chicago Press.

Russell Sage Foundation. 2003. "Future of Work" Working Group, document available at: *www.russellsage.org/programs/proj_reviews/incarceration.htm.*

Sabol, William J., and James P. Lynch. 1997. "Crime Policy Report: Did Getting Tough on Crime Pay?" Washington, D.C.: Urban Institute.

Sampson, Robert J., and John H. Laub. 1995. "Crime and Deviance over the Life Course: The Salience of Adult Social Bonds." *American Sociological Review* 55(5): 609–27.

Schaenman, R. 1995. Letter to the editor. *New York Times,* February 6.

Sherman, Larry, Denise Gottfredson, Doris Mackenzie, John Eck, Peter Reuter, and Shawn Bushway. 1997. "Preventing Crime: What Works, What Doesn't, and What's Promising." Report to Congress, National Institute of Justice (Washington, D.C.). Available at: *www.ncjrs.org/works.*

Snell, Tracy L. 1995. *Correctional Populations in the United States, 1993.* Bureau of Justice Statistics publication no. NCJ-156241. Washington: U.S. Department of Justice.

Spencer, Margaret B., and Carol Markstrom-Adams. 1990. "Identity Processes Among Racial and Ethnic Minority Children." *Child Development* 61: 290–310.

Stanton, Ann M. 1980. *When Mothers Go to Jail.* Lexington, Mass.: Lexington Books.

Sutherland, Edwin H. 1973. *On Analyzing Crime.* Chicago: University of Chicago Press.

Tonry, Michael. 1995. *Malign Neglect—Race, Crime, and Punishment in America.* New York: Oxford.

Tucker, Belinda M., and Ronald J. Taylor. 1989. "Demographic Correlates of Relationship Status Among Black Americans." *Journal of Marriage and the Family* 51: 655–65.

U.S. Bureau of the Census. 1992. *Marriage, Divorce and Remarriage in the 1990's.* Current Population Reports, series P-23, no. 180. Washington: U.S. Government Printing Office.

Valentine, Betty Lou. 1978. *Hustling and Other Hard Work.* New York: Free Press.

Vigil, J. D. 1989. "Street Socialization, Locura Behavior, and Violence Among Chicago Gang Members." In *Proceedings: Research Conference on Violence and Homicide in Hispanic Communities,* edited by J. Kraus, S. Sorenson, and P. Juarez. Los Angeles: University of California Press.

Viscusi, W. K. 1986. "The Valuations of Risks to Life and Health: Guidelines for Policy Analysis." In *Benefits Assessment, the State of the Art,* edited by Judith Bentkover, Vincent Covello, and Jeryl Mumpower. Dordrecht, Holland: Reidel Publishing.

Western, Bruce. 2001. "The Impact of Incarceration on Wage Mobility and Inequality." *American Sociological Review* 67: 477–98.

Western, Bruce, and Becky Pettit. 2000. "Incarceration and Racial Inequality in Men's Employment." *Industrial and Labor Relations Review* 54(1): 3–16.

Wilson, William J. 1987. *The Truly Disadvantaged.* Chicago: University of Chicago Press.

# PART III

## Contemporary Issues of Fatherhood

# Chapter 6

## BUILDING A FATHERHOOD MOVEMENT IN SOUTH CAROLINA

### BARBARA MORRISON-RODRIGUEZ

This chapter describes the efforts made in South Carolina to place the issue of father absence and its relationship to poverty on the social agenda. It delineates the key role played by a faith-based philanthropy in spearheading this effort through a strategic partnership with the academic community and the people of South Carolina. It describes and proposes an approach to strategic grant making that not only has special relevance for father engagement activities but that also can serve as a model for addressing many different types of human needs.

### POVERTY IN SOUTH CAROLINA AND ITS RELATIONSHIP TO FATHER ABSENCE

The Sisters of Charity Foundation of South Carolina decided to make father absence a programmatic focus when its role in promoting and maintaining poverty was suggested by empirical research. As a foundation committed to serving the poor, its first task for new grant-making activities was to commission a review and written report on the root causes of poverty and their consequences in the state of South Carolina. Several predictable factors were identified: low educational attainment by the adult population, poor health status, lack of a skilled workforce prepared for new jobs, low wage rates, and cultural, behavioral and attitudinal factors that predisposed people to be born into or live in poverty.

Among the behavioral factors was the strong association between family structure and poverty among children. Specifically, the rates of poverty were significantly higher for children in a household headed by unmarried females—father-absent households.

A few key statistics led this faith-based foundation to claim as its niche the promotion of programs and activities to strengthen families with special attention to reducing poverty through father engagement. These key statistics for South Carolina indicated the following:

- In 1994, 13.2 percent of white infants and 57.8 percent of black infants were born to unmarried mothers.

- The rate of marriage declined from 22.3 per 1,000 adults in 1970 to 14.1 per 1,000 adults in 1994.

- The median income for families with the father present is more than three times that of families headed by a single female.

- Sixty-nine percent of families in poverty are headed by single mothers.

- Among the forty-six counties in South Carolina, half had rates of father-absent households that exceed 262 per 1,000 households, or 26 percent.

- For every indicator of material poverty and social dysfunction (teen pregnancy, out-of-wedlock births, school dropout, violent crime, juvenile crime, and welfare dependency), rates were highest in those counties with the highest rates of father absence.[1]

Alarmed by the data and determined to attack this aspect of poverty frequently neglected by or exacerbated by misguided social welfare policy, the foundation decided to mount a major initiative to reengage fathers in the lives of South Carolina's children. One of its first tasks was to forge partnerships to further analyze the problem, develop a plan for strategic action, and initiate a planning process.

### FORGING A PARTNERSHIP: THE FOUNDATION, THE UNIVERSITY, AND COMMUNITIES

Seeding a father-engagement movement in South Carolina required the energy and commitment of three partners: (1) the Sisters of Charity Foundation, operating out of a moral framework to address the needs of the poor and support healthy families and communities across the state, (2) an academic partner, the University of South Carolina, who shared a similar commitment to strengthening families and communities through applied social research and policy analysis, and (3) concerned communities across South Carolina who determined that the crisis of family dissolution and resulting material and spiritual poverty required immediate attention.

### The Foundation and Its Role

The Sisters of Charity Foundation is what is known as a conversion foundation. It was created and funded when the Sisters of Charity of St. Augustine and its CSA (Catholic Sisters of St. Augustine) Health System formed a new partnership with Columbia/HCA Healthcare Corporation in 1995 to provide integrated health care that preserved and strengthened the provision of health care by entities affiliated with the Catholic church. The order operated health services at two Ohio sites, Cleveland and Canton, and in the state of South Carolina. Columbia/HCA purchased a 50 percent interest in the health systems in each site, resulting in conversion foundations in each site with $82.5 million for the South Carolina foundation. Thus, the foundation brings to the partnership considerable financial resources.

As important as its financial resources—if not more so—is the moral leadership that the foundation has played in the father-engagement initiative because of its long-held commitment to meeting the needs of the poor within a Catholic moral philosophy. The Sisters of Charity Foundation of South Carolina seeks to be a good and faithful servant. In keeping with the social teachings of the Catholic church and the mission of the Sisters of Charity of St. Augustine, the foundation uses its resources and endeavors to mobilize the resources of others to confront the fundamental causes of poverty and reduce its impact in South Carolina. As a value-driven organization, the foundation is committed to addressing the needs of the poor and underserved by understanding the root causes of poverty, nurturing the growth of healthy communities, emphasizing youth and family, and measuring outcomes of these efforts.

The foundation espouses and practices strategic grant making by challenging itself to understand, advocate, participate, and cooperate with other public and private entities equally concerned with the eradication of poverty. Awarding dollars for program development is only one of several strategies it uses to reduce poverty. Public education through partnerships with the press, education of key policy makers through educational seminars, and education of other philanthropic organizations are among is strategies.

Strategic grant making structures a grants program around what the grant maker wants to effect and the impact the grant maker seeks rather than simply concentrating on individual grants. Grants are a tool to reach the goals of the grant maker, rather than ends in themselves. Strategic grant making is predicated on careful planning before any grants are made. Thus, the role of the foundation in the partnership is that of strategic funder and moral compass for the initiative to reduce poverty through father engagement. In its role as moral compass, the foundation's approach was shaped by two uncompromising moral positions.

The first was to *unapologetically affirm that children should be born into intact families headed by married parents.* In taking this position, the foundation acknowledged that its overall interest in reducing poverty would mean that its principal target population would be low-income noncustodial fathers, many (if not most) of whom would not be married to the mother(s) of their child(ren). It also recognized that attempting to force fathers to marry or explicitly holding out marriage as a program outcome was not advisable. Nevertheless, in articulating guiding principles for programs that it funded, it emphasized the sanctity of marriage and preparation for married life as important foci for program activities with fathers. The second, and related, moral premise was that of *redemptive relationships,* meaning that essentially, no matter what circumstances caused the disconnection between the father and his children, the goal of programs should be to foster healthy reconnections in a spirit of forgiveness, including reconnections to the mother and her extended family when it was in the best interest of the child.

### The University and Its Role

The initial relationship between the Sisters of Charity Foundation and the University of South Carolina (USC) began before father engagement as an area for strategic grant making had been decided on. Staff from the university's Institute for Families in Society (IFS) were requested to be part of the research and development team formed by the foundation to conduct research and write an analytic report on poverty in South Carolina, titled "Dimensions of Poverty." This work resulted in the foundation's placing father absence high on its list of priorities. This early alliance set the stage for the institute's leadership in the father-engagement initiative.

The Institute for Families in Society is a unique academic entity. IFS seeks to enhance family well-being through interdisciplinary research, education, and consultation at the community, state, national, and international levels. Conceived as a partnership between the University of South Carolina and the broader community, the IFS was planned in collaboration with representatives from public and private agencies. The main theme of the institute's work is the need to enhance connections between family members and between families and their communities. IFS studies the needs of families in a changing society, stimulates development of services and policies responsive to those needs, evaluates the effects of programs and policies on children and families, and consults with policy makers and communities about ways to strengthen neighborhoods and enhance family well-being.

In its efforts to stimulate greater attention to family issues in both the university and the community, the institute facilitates collaboration within the university and between it and leaders in government, private agencies, business, and voluntary civic, religious, and philanthropic organizations. Its staff consists of sixty principal faculty from a variety of academic disciplines and one hundred affiliated faculty and policy fellows. The faculty is advised by a council of corporate and philanthropic leaders, community leaders, state legislators, state agency directors, and leaders in the bar and the judiciary.

The institute's role in the father-engagement initiative has been to

- provide guidance to the Sisters of Charity Foundation on its strategic grant making generally and with regard to father engagement in particular

- review and synthesize research on the relationship between father absence, poverty, and other social indicators nationally and in South Carolina

- review and synthesize information on guiding principles and best practices in the fatherhood field for use in educating the foundation's board, providing technical assistance to its grantees, and educating the public and the press

- educate the foundation board on the relationship between father absence and poverty and the role that private philanthropy can play in addressing related problems

- provide intensive and ongoing technical assistance to grantees in planning, program development and implementation, and empowerment evaluation

- evaluate the strategic grant-making efforts of the foundation related to father engagement

## COMMUNITIES AND THEIR ROLE

The roles we envisioned for communities were those of planners, program designers, and service providers. In order to execute these roles, communities needed to be knowledgeable about the correlates and consequences of father absence in their particular locale. They needed data. It was felt that communities needed to be made aware of this information and its significance for the state in general and for their communities in particular.

Further, communities needed to be aware of best practices in the fatherhood field. They needed a set of guiding principles to frame their intervention efforts, technical assistance and skill building in planning, coalition building, program design, and evaluation methodology.

As our work progressed, it became very clear that communities and their leaders had long been concerned about the decline in marriage, increases in out-of-wedlock births, and the apparent abdication of responsibility by many fathers for their children. But they were overwhelmed by the enormity of the problem, their sense of helplessness obvious from the frequently expressed the opinion that "somebody should do something" about the problem.

The goal became to convince communities that the "somebody" was them and the "something" was to create partnerships at the local level to reengage fathers. A detailed strategy was planned and executed to make this case.

## FATHER ENGAGEMENT: ONE APPROACH TO STARTING A MOVEMENT

The father-engagement initiative was an effort to put the concept of strategic grant making into action. The foundation wished to be very thoughtful in how it used its funds to foster father engagement. As a starting point, it identified several preparatory goals:

• analyze the existing research on the correlates and consequences of father absence and synthesize it in a manner most useful for planning and program development;

• educate its board in all aspects of the issue and the relationship between father absence and poverty so as to assure board members that investment in this program area was consistent with the foundation's mission;

• draw on the expert opinion and advice of the key leaders and experienced practitioners in the fatherhood field; and

• create a public consciousness of the problem of father absence in South Carolina so as to generate interest and create a climate receptive to strategic action.

**Analysis of Related Research and Literature**

Members of the faculty of the Institute for Families in Society were paid by the foundation to do a comprehensive review of the literature on father absence, with special attention to its relationship to poverty. Their findings were synthesized and formed the front half of a request for proposal document (RFP), which was used as an educational tool for potential grantees and the public at large. The RFP presented and explained the relationship of father absence to child poverty, lower educational attainment, decreased mental health, higher rates of serious juvenile crime, higher rates of teen pregnancy, and higher rates of child maltreatment, as well as its negative impact on adult women and adult men, especially those who are absent fathers. In the process, several websites were identified that would be sources of valuable information for grantees, and a list of these websites was included in the technical assistance package for them. A comprehensive reading list and bibliography were also developed for use by the foundation board, the public, and potential grantees. Foundation and institute staff also made site visits to fatherhood programs mentioned in the literature as exemplary models.

The review of the related literature was useful for identifying principles to guide program development. Of special importance was the work of W. J. Doherty, E. F. Kouneski, and M. E. Erickson (1996), who recommended principles for father-engagement programs that were incorporated into the RFP:

- Target all the domains of responsible fathering that need reme-diation or enhancement: paternity, presence, economic support and involvement.

- Involve mothers where feasible.

- Promote the well-being of mothers and the mother-father relationship.

- Take into account the influence of mother's and father's family of origin.

- Emphasize critical transition points for fathers and children.

- Include an employment component.

To this set of principles the foundation added a few more cited in the literature:

- Effective programs must reach the "heart of the father."

- Effective programs must deal with the emotions of men, with their relationships with their own fathers, and with their feelings about themselves as men and as fathers to their own children.

### Education of the Foundation Board

The foundation's board of directors needed to be convinced that the foundation should invest in father-engagement strategies. Informa-tion derived from research and expert opinion were used to make this case. Such educational efforts also meant that the board and its program committee would be more informed and thereby better able to judge the quality of grant applications and to make wise funding decisions. Board education sessions were held where the research was presented and experts from the field such as David Blankenhorn, author of *Fatherless America*, and Ron Mincy, director of fatherhood programs for the Ford Foundation, were invited to speak to board members. Key board members, like the chair of the program com-mittee, were taken on field trips to visit active and exemplary father-hood programs in several states. No other data source made so profound an impression as did the site visits. These members became converts to the cause and helped to make the case with still skeptical colleagues on the board.

### The Counsel of Experts

Experts drawn from the fatherhood movement in the United States were solicited to sit on two advisory panels and provide feedback on the draft RFP. One panel, composed of national leaders in the fatherhood movement in the United States, helped to frame issues within a policy and political context and guide us in our strategic efforts to garner political support for the initiative and to educate the public. The second panel, made up of practitioners running father-engagement programs, suggested areas pertinent to technical assistance, processing information for consumption by community grass roots organizations, and setting realistic parameters about startup, program capacity, and outcomes. We also drew on this practitioners' panel for guest speakers at regional workshops. Nothing provides as much motivation to join the fatherhood movement as seeing and interacting with providers in the trenches who add an element of enthusiasm grounded in reality.

### Creating Public Conscience: Strategic Use of the RFP

The RFP was used to educate the public as well as potential grantees. Once it was finalized it was attractively formatted, printed, and mailed to seven thousand people across the state, including politicians, policy makers, state agency heads, community leaders, churches, men's and youth organizations, schools, public human service organizations, and nonprofit organizations. Other state foundations were targeted as well with the hope that they would be encouraged to fund similar efforts.

### The Press as Collaborators

Copies of the RFP were sent to the editors of major newspapers around the state. At a meeting with the editorial board of *The State*, the largest newspaper in South Carolina, further data on father absence in the state were provided. Ideas were suggested for editorials on father absence. The press also assisted in advertising planned regional workshops for potential grantees and other interested parties, funded by the foundation. A series of editorials and articles on father absence and the importance of fathers to families appeared in several newspapers around the state, generating considerable interest in the initiative.

### Regional Workshops

Institute faculty designed, planned, and carried out four regional day-long workshops, in Florence, Columbia, Spartanburg, and Charleston. Over five hundred people registered for the workshops with an approximately 70 percent attendance rate. The morning session was geared to all attendees whether they intended to apply for a grant or were just there to be educated on the issue. The agenda for the morning included background on the foundation and its proactive grant making, as well as its vision for the fatherhood initiative; highlights of the relevant research; presentation of the moral framework and guiding program principles; and introduction of the concept of empowerment evaluation and its role in the initiative. Included in the morning session was a presentation by a practitioner working with men in a father-engagement program. These presentations generated a great deal of excitement. Packets were provided that contained bibliographies, websites, and resource information that could be used by communities to initiate their planning efforts. There was some local press coverage.

Lunch was provided for the participants, and this was an opportunity for people to begin to network around their shared interest in the topic. In some cases, participants who lived and worked in the same geographic area did not know each other. The workshops provided further opportunities for making connections. The regional workshops spawned several coalitions that carried through the planning and program development phases of the initiative.

The afternoon session was geared to the needs of potential grantees. The RFP was discussed in detail, including the requirements for funding, the availability and types of technical assistance to be provided, and the criteria by which applications would be judged. Particular attention was paid to the role of evaluation in the process and the expectations for grantees to invest fully in the evaluation process.

### The Grants Makers Network

Father absence is such a significant issue in South Carolina that it is unlikely that any one entity can provide sufficient leadership and financial support for intervention efforts. Both the scope of activities and long-term sustainability depend on enlisting others to join the nascent movement. The Sisters of Charity Foundation met with the South Carolina Grants Makers Network to educate them about the issue of father absence and its relationship to poverty and to encourage them to invest some of their funds in similar efforts. Plans are on the drawing board to connect with other foundations in the southeastern region of the United States who share an interest in this topic or could be encouraged to do so.

## GETTING COMMUNITIES GEARED UP

### Phase 1: Planning

The foundation took a strategic step rarely seen in philanthropic funding by funding planning on a competitive basis to communities wishing to develop a father-engagement strategy at the local level. Communities were invited to apply for a $1,500 planning grant to help facilitate the formation of a community collaborative and conduct community forums to examine issues and make recommendations over an eight-week planning period. Because of the complexity of the problems disconnected fathers encounter, it was felt that no single agency in the community could mount a father-engagement program alone. Collaborations were not only encouraged, they were required; the ability of applicants to put together an effective collaborative effort became one criterion against which applications were judged.

Sixty-six groups applied for planning grants, and twenty-one grants were awarded. The application for a planning grant required attention to several areas:

- a description of the planning process to be used

- identification of the key facilitators, their experience, and their expertise

- identification and description of the community groups and organizations who would form the local father-engagement coalition and the specific role they would play in the initiative

- a description of current or past efforts in the community to work with men on fatherhood issues

- identification of resources needed for planning and of resources that could be leveraged

- description of basic information about the community, with special attention to factors and patterns correlated with father absence

- types of fathers who would be the target population for planning and programming, with a supporting rationale for their selection

Applicants' handling of these elements gave an indication of how serious the community and applicant was about addressing father absence and whether there was a solid nexus of leadership to generate planned activity.

### Phase 2: Intensive Technical Assistance to Grantees

Institute faculty have provided intensive technical assistance to grantees from the start of this initiative and will continue to do so for current and future grantees. Technical assistance has been provided in several day-long sessions with community coalitions receiving planning grants and those invited to submit full program proposals. Regular follow-up telephone consultation and review and comment of written drafts of proposals have all been provided, with particular attention to "leveling the playing field" so that the smallest grassroots groups could compete with more sophisticated applicants. In addition to the special technical assistance that applicants request, all applicants are to receive technical assistance in the following areas from the institute or other contracted trainers:

- community profiling using geographic information systems (GIS) and other data to coordinate indicators related to father absence, poverty, and social disorganization

- coaching through the planning process

- assistance with program design and implementation

- help with participant targeting, recruitment, and retention strategies

- evaluation design and implementation

- fiscal management of operational expenditures and auditing functions for grants management

- preparation of quarterly and year-end reports

**Phase 3: Program Development**

Communities submitted reports on their planning efforts. Of the twenty-one groups receiving planning grants, eleven were invited to submit further, fully developed program-design applications, in which they would fully describe the target population with relevant profiling data; articulate a program vision with related program goals, activities, and outcomes for the three-year project period; refine the description of the leadership; specify the program partners and the specific roles they would play in the program (letters of commitment were required); outline strategies for participant recruitment and retention; identify potential risks and how they would be managed; provide a three-year line-item budget; and spell out initial plans for long-term sustainability of the program. Each program funded was to receive a total of $360,000 for a three-year period, continued funding to be based on empirically demonstrated achievement of outcomes as articulated by the grantees themselves.

This intensive process resulted in six funded programs representing an investment of $2.2 million by the Sisters of Charity Foundation (see appendix A for a description of the six funded programs). Applicants were judged by Foundation and Institute staff and also by the panel of experienced practitioners in the fatherhood field. Because South Carolina is 38 percent African American and the focus is on reducing poverty, the majority of those served by all of these programs will be African American men and their children. Although there are certainly many poor white disconnected fathers in South Carolina, no applications were received that target this population.

Although five programs that submitted detailed program-design application were not funded in the first cycle, they are considered fundable with some additional technical assistance and are a priority for funding in the second round. The foundation is considering initiating a third round of funding by going back to the other forty-five communities of the sixty-six that initially competed for planning grants and by approaching workshop attendees to encourage them to apply. We believe that this approach serves as a model for strategic grant making and community-capacity building that can be used in all efforts to improve family and community life.

### Evaluation from the Start

Program evaluation, an important aspect of the father-engagement project, is taking place on several levels. First, evaluation forms were completed by all participants attending the workshops and receiving technical assistance of any kind. This allowed the foundation to determine whether its investment in these aspects of the strategic grant making were worthwhile. The evaluations have been overwhelmingly positive.

In conjunction with community psychology doctoral students at USC, a workbook entitled *Evaluation from the Start* was developed for work with community groups. A special version of it was created with exemplars for father-engagement programs.[2] The workbook is designed to explain the purpose of evaluation and evaluation methodology in a user-friendly manner that demystifies the process for lay audiences. It is founded on the principles of empowerment evaluation, in which communities and their program providers take ownership of the evaluation process by articulating their own program vision, from which self-defined goals, action strategies, outcomes, and benchmarks emerge. Program staff participate in the collection and analysis of both process and outcome data. Professional evaluators serve as teachers and technical advisers. Institute faculty are assisting grantees with identification of specific instruments for measuring some of their outcomes, while encouraging the use of the same or similar instruments across programs to make it possible to compare outcomes of different approaches to father engagement.

### CONCLUSION

Much of the activity in the fatherhood movement had been funded and shaped by large organizations such as the Ford Foundation who have made major investments in this area. Smaller local foundations have played a smaller but significant role. There is clearly a role for faith-based philanthropies in this movement. Although many philanthropies do not have the resources of the Sisters of Charity Foundation, their moral leadership is as important as their financial contribution to the movement. At the core of disconnections between men and their families are profound moral and value conflicts. All of the problem cannot be explained solely by economic influences. Within the African American community, material poverty has been a sad and constant aspect of life. Yet the crisis in relationships between black men and women and between black fathers and their children is unprecedented. We must be fearless in the discussion of issues such as marriage, sexual responsibility, and parental obligations.

## APPENDIX A:

Father-Engagement Programs in South Carolina Funded by the Sisters of Charity Foundation of South Carolina in November 1998

## OUR FATHER INITIATIVE

Georgetown County

### Collaborative Partners

Georgetown County United Way

Georgetown County Detention Center

St. Cyprian's Catholic Church Parenting and Resource Center

St. Cyprian's Outreach Center

Baskerville Youth Ministries

### Target Population

Intervention and treatment: Twenty-five fathers at the Georgetown Detention Center incarcerated for nonpayment of child support and the estimated thirty-eight women who are their partners or the mothers of their children and the children.
Prevention: 245 youths.

### Program Overview

Program has a three-pronged approach. "Treatment" phase for incarcerated fathers and their children through prison-based fathering programs, while mothers and children are assisted simultaneously by St. Cyprian's Parenting Resource Center. Both to prepare for successful coparenting and follow-up upon release of the father. "Intervention" phase targets men in the community who are experiencing difficulty in their fathering roles. All fathers will receive individual and peer counseling, job preparation and job placement, spiritual counseling, and recreational activities with children. "Prevention" phase targets youth in Georgetown county to encourage personal responsibility, abstinence or responsible sexual behavior, and pro-marriage and family values.

## FATHER ENGAGEMENT

Florence and Marion Counties

### Collaborative Partners

Telamon Employment Training and Job Placement Program

Pee Dee Catholic Charities

Pee Dee Coalition Against Domestic Violence

Pee Dee Boys and Girls Clubs

Family Court

Florence and Marion Departments of Social Services

### Target Population

Low income, unemployed or underemployed, noncustodial unwed fathers ages eighteen to twenty-four.

### Program Overview

Fathers will receive two hundred hours of male parenting classes in conjunction with eight hundred hours of paid construction and carpentry skills training. Individual, peer group, and spiritual counseling. Program curriculum includes topics such as building one's faith, facing one's past, stress and anger management, violence and conflict resolution, sobriety, child care, educational opportunities, credit counseling and money management, and personal goal setting. Structured activities to foster father-child interaction and bonding.

This program has been designated by the judicial system as an alternative to incarceration for fathers with outstanding child-support obligations.

## FATHER TO FATHER

North Charleston

### Collaborative Partners

Florence Crittenton (program for unmarried mothers)

The Cannon Street YMCA

The Christian Family YMCA

St. Peter's African Methodist Episcopal Church

Counseling Center of Charleston

Boy Scouts of America (Operation First Class)

### Target Population

Unmarried, noncustodial fathers between the ages of eighteen and fifty. Two hundred fifty boys, seventeen to eighteen years of age in severely distressed neighborhoods.

### Program Overview

To reduce the likelihood of fathering before marriage, Operation First Class, a scouting program for low-income boys, will focus on achievement of the Family Life Merit Badge. This program features an abstinence-based human sexuality course, money and budgeting skills, and parenting skills with a strong emphasis on personal values and character building. It will also provide leadership opportunities for the men enrolled in "Father to Father" to mentor these boys. The Father to Father program is a twenty-four-week structured peer-support format. Weekly sessions focus on topics such as anger management, communication skills, coparenting, job readiness, and spiritual education. Prayer, meditation, group bonding between fathers, and structured father-child activities are aspects of the program. Legal services are provided to assist with paternity establishment and child-support obligations. Graduates of the program will be trained to become paid peer facilitators for future programming cycles.

## ACTIVE FATHERS MAKING A DIFFERENCE
Lake City and Georgetown

### Collaborative Partners
Pee Dee Star Consortium

### Target Population
Teen and young adult fathers, ages thirteen to twenty-three, some of whom are still in school. The population will focus on low-income non-custodial fathers who lack marketable skills and who have not yet established paternity.

### Program Overview
Program components include structured father-child activities, child development, coparenting, time management, stress management, child discipline, conflict resolution, spiritual counseling, and intergenerational relationships. A major focus of the program is to help fathers complete their education and become prepared for the job market. A "buddy system" between upstanding men in the community and fathers in the program is featured. This is the most grassroots initiative with leadership based in the faith community.

## FATHERS MATTER
Fairfield County (very rural)

### Collaborative Partners
Fairfield County Substance Abuse Commission

Good Samaritan House (Homeless Shelter)

Clemson University Extension Services

Calvary Presbyterian Church

South Carolina Department of Health and Environmental Control (DHEC)

**Target Population**

Noncustodial low-income fathers between the ages of twenty and thirty-five who wish to be involved in the lives of their children.

**Program Overview**

The program will provide job assistance and job coaching by accessing training funds under welfare reform for noncustodial parents. Job preparedness will also include adult literacy classes, job training through vocational rehabilitation services, and micro-enterprise skills. Peer mentoring and structured father-child activities are planned. Curriculum includes communication skills, coparenting, personal care, and healthy life style. Fathers will be provided with health screenings as a way to detect unaddressed medical and addiction problems. An innovative feature of this program is creation of a father-child gospel choir for men enrolled in the program.

**VOORHEES COLLEGE PARTNERSHIP FOR EMPOWERING FATHERS**

Bamberg County

**Collaborative Partners**

Voorhees College (a historically Black land-grant college)

Mt. Carmel United Methodist Church

Bamberg County Ministerial Alliance

Bamberg County Department of Mental Health

Low Country Health Start (infant mortality reduction program)

Denmark-Olar Teen Life Center

Concerned Fathers of Bamberg County

South Carolina Department of Juvenile Justice

Bamberg County Department of Social Services

## Target Population

Noncustodial fathers between the ages of seventeen and forty and teenage males between the ages of ten and seventeen for the prevention program

## Program Overview

The curriculum of this program will focus on anger management, male and female relationships, men's issues with their families of origin, substance abuse, self-development, communications skills, literacy, human sexuality and responsible sexual behavior, and child development. Spiritual counseling and emotional peer support will be provided to all fathers, as well as health screening, medical services, and recreational activities for the men as a group and for fathers and their children, and legal services related to paternity establishment and child-support obligations. The prevention component is based on a Rites of Passage curriculum for African American males.

## NOTES

1. For a more detailed analysis of these see Palmetto Family Council (1994).
2. Information on the Evaluation from the Start workbook can be obtained from Dr. Irene Luckey, Project Evaluator, Institute for Families in Society, University of South Carolina, Columbia, SC 29208, (803) 737-3191, irenel@ss1.csd.sc.edu.

## REFERENCES

Doherty, W. J., E. F. Kouneski, and M. E. Erickson. 1996. "Responsible Fathering: An Overview and Conceptual Framework." Report. Washington, D.C.: Administration for Children and Families, Office of the Assistant Secretary for Planning and Evaluation, U.S. Department of Health and Human Services.

Palmetto Family Council. 1994. "Father Absence: A South Carolina Crisis." Palmetto, S.C.: Palmetto Family Council.

# Chapter 7

## FATHERLESSNESS IN AFRICAN AMERICAN FAMILIES: PRIMARY, SECONDARY, AND TERTIARY PREVENTION

### WORNIE L. REED

The increasing rate of father absence in the homes of many African American children presents numerous challenges. It may be instructive to examine the different approaches that are used to address this issue. I will use a public health model to examine the problematic nature of the ways many programs approach the issue of African American fathers and families—specifically, how the public health intervention-prevention framework is used to analyze various approaches to address "fatherlessness" and the potential successes and failures of some of these approaches. This analysis is informed by my experience as an evaluator for some of these programs and my participation in various forums on the issue.

The public health framework first defines a health issue in terms of its nature, extent, and distribution in a geographically defined area and then develops approaches to the problem using three levels of prevention: primary prevention, secondary prevention, and tertiary prevention. Tertiary prevention is applied to individuals who already have the problem; attempts are made to ameliorate or remedy the problem. In disease, tertiary prevention is medical treatment of the affected individual. For example, persons with heart disease are treated to keep them from becoming sicker.

Secondary prevention is given to individuals who are at risk of having the problem, addressing the at-risk status of specific individuals. In the example of heart disease, secondary prevention strategies are aimed at persons at risk of developing heart disease because they smoke, have high blood pressure, or have a family history of the disease.

Primary prevention is aimed at the general population. It seeks to prevent individuals from acquiring the at-risk status as well as the actual condition. In the example of heart disease, primary prevention may consist of educational measures such as warning the general public about the risk factors of smoking, hereditary factors, and poor diet. My use of this model does not mean that I am defining fatherlessness as a public health issue. Rather, I am using the public health prevention-intervention model as a framework for discussing the fatherlessness issue.

The problem here is "fatherlessness"—African American families and homes without resident fathers and the status of being an absent father. On average all children suffer when they spend parts of their child and teenage years without their father in the family (McLanahan and Bumpass 1988; McLanahan and Sandefur 1994; Jaynes and Williams 1989; Dawson 1991; Angel and Angel 1993; Zill and Schoenborn 1990).

Children who grow up in a household with only one biological parent are worse off, *on average,* than children who grow up in a household with both of their biological parents, regardless of whether the parents are married when the child is born, and regardless of whether the resident parent remarries (McLanahan and Sandefur 1994).

Compared with teenagers of similar background who grow up with both parents at home, adolescents who have lived apart from one of their parents during some period of childhood are twice as likely to drop out of school or have a child before age twenty, and they are one and a half times as likely to be idle—out of school and out of work—in their late teens and early twenties (McLanahan and Sandefur 1994).

Does this mean that single motherhood and absence of the father are therefore the root cause of poor child outcomes, such as school failure and juvenile delinquency? Of course not. Although living with just one parent increases a child's risk of experiencing all of these negative outcomes, it is not the only or even the major cause. Growing up with a single parent is just one among many factors that put children at risk of failure, just as lack of exercise is only one among many factors that put people at risk for heart disease. Many individuals who do not exercise never suffer a heart attack, and many children raised by single mothers grow up to be quite successful.

However, fatherlessness does put many children at risk, and African American children suffer more than the general population of children because on average they tend to have more fatherlessness and fewer resources to counter the overriding effects of fatherlessness. Even among two-parent families, African American children experience more of these negative outcomes than white children, and the situation is exacerbated for children in families headed by a single woman. On average they have fewer family and community resources to support them.

## TERTIARY PREVENTION AND INTERVENTION

Fatherlessness in African American communities is addressed in several ways. Many programs focus on single females who are heading households. Increasingly, however, attention is focused on the men who are absent fathers.

Much of the work of intervening with fathers takes place at the tertiary level, males who already have the problem because they are absent fathers. Such fathers are usually estranged from the mother and child. Efforts are made to reconnect them, with considerable emphasis on father-child bonding and the encouragement of greater male parenting responsibilities.

In 1997 fifty-one "fathering practitioners" from around the nation convened in Cleveland to share their "best practices" experiences in addressing absent fatherhood, mostly on the tertiary level. They noted that successful programs combined at least three components: personal development, father development, and employment-related skill-building services. Unfortunately, few programs have all three of these elements. In addition, building skills without providing jobs at the end of the training is a problematic aspect of many programs.

At the Urban Child Research Center at Cleveland State University we evaluated a program that could be categorized as operating at the tertiary level of prevention, and was designed to have all three of the components of successful programs. Low-income fathers, most of them African American, who were out of work or who had a problematic relationship with their children or the children's mother were recruited into the program. They attended twice-weekly workshops that were designed to enhance personal development and produce a sense of responsibility toward family, which was expected to cause these fathers to reconnect with their children and possibly their children's mother. It was expected that this would in turn result in the men's greater tendency to get and hold jobs. A key element in this program was the presence of a job developer who actually developed contacts and placed men in jobs.

The results of the project were mixed. On the one hand the workshops did create a greater sense of family relationships within a significant proportion of the men. On the other hand, many of the men were interested in the program only to the extent of acquiring a job. Despite this interest, however, some of the men did not remain in their newly acquired jobs, and seemed to have difficulty fitting into some work situations. In response, the job developer advocated for the participation of a social worker to counsel these men and help them develop work-related psycho-social skills. This ongoing counseling was seen as a necessary feature of the employment-related skill-building services.

## SECONDARY PREVENTION

Some of the work of intervening with fathers takes place at the secondary level of prevention, addressing at-risk males. African American males who do not have stable jobs, who have not finished high school, who are substance abusers, who have poor health, or who are in or are at risk for being in the criminal justice system have meager potential means of taking care of their children. The likelihood of such men being able to form or maintain an intact family would be relatively low. Some bold programs attempt to intervene with such men. The successful ones recognize that for many of these men, the problems come in bundles—solving one problem often depends upon recognizing and solving a second or third problem. Consequently, some well-designed programs seek to arrange for a coordination of services. We evaluated one such program.

The program set about to intervene with African American males in a predominantly black community of 25,000 residents which had a poverty rate of over 60 percent. Initially the program had five objectives: increased access to health care, increased employment opportunities, improved educational performance, improved encounters with the criminal justice system, and increased interaction and collaboration among agencies addressing issues related to the first four objectives. This was quite ambitious for one program, so with the consent of the funding agency most energy was eventually directed toward the fifth objective, developing effective interaction and collaboration among agencies. This secondary level of prevention addressed the issue of fatherlessness indirectly: as these men go, so go the families in this neighborhood.

Two key lessons were learned from this project: the necessity for efficient referral systems between agencies, and the difficulty of establishing interagency collaborations when such activity has low priority in agencies that are not structured or financed to do so. Often, one agency's success with a client is dependent upon the success of another agency. For example, some job training programs require participants to have a high school diploma or a G.E.D. To prevent the client from falling through the cracks, a coordinated referral to a G.E.D. program may be necessary.

### PRIMARY PREVENTION

Considerable attention has been given to primary prevention of fatherlessness, where the emphasis is on preventing the at-risk situations. However, some of these efforts are problematic in that they fail to use approaches that consider the interconnectedness of the African American "fatherlessness" with social and economic trends and social forces and social policies. There is often a confusion between "cures" and "causes," between successful remedies and how the problem developed in the first place. For example, some service providers make erroneous extrapolations from their work in helping black men to turn their life around by building their self-esteem. They assume that because some black males are successfully transformed in such programs that the *lack* of self-esteem is the cause of the men being in their situation in the first place. Working on building self-esteem may be a useful secondary prevention strategy, but not an appropriate primary prevention strategy.

### FOCUSING UPSTREAM

A story told in public health circles goes as follows: Two physicians standing beside a swiftly flowing river hear a cry for help from a drowning person. One physician jumps in, swims to the person calling for help, brings him ashore, and the two physicians apply artificial respiration. Soon a second cry for help is heard and the second physician jumps in, pulls the second victim to shore, and applies artificial respiration. A third cry is heard, and the process is repeated. At this point one of the physicians says to the other, "You stay here and rescue the next one. I'm going upstream to see who's pushing these people in."

Obviously tertiary prevention—tending to those afflicted by the problem, be it drowning, heart disease, or fatherlessness—is necessary, but there is also a need for primary and secondary prevention. *Preventing* the condition has been called "focusing upstream." Focusing upstream requires us to expand our analysis of the situation of black family fatherlessness. The work of sociologists from W. E. B. Du Bois over a century ago to Andrew Billingsley in the 1960s to Robert Hill in the 1990s provide orientations for this analysis.

### HOLISTIC FRAMEWORK

Du Bois (1898) proposed that the proper study of black individuals and families required a holistic approach. He contended that the proper understanding of black Americans was achieved through assessing the influence of historical, cultural, social, economic, and political forces that had determined the circumstances of their lives. This holistic approach was employed in his two pioneering studies, *The Philadelphia Negro* (1967 [1899]) and *The Negro American Family* (1970 [1908]).

Andrew Billingsley used Du Bois's holistic approach in his social systems formulation (1968). Using Talcott Parsons's social systems approach (Parsons 1951, Parsons and Bales 1955), Billingsley described the black family as a social system imbedded in wider social systems:

> The Negro family is imbedded in a network of mutually interdependent relationships with the Negro community and the wider society. The Negro community includes within itself a number of institutions which may also be viewed as subsystems. The wider society consists of major institutions which help set the conditions for Negro family life. Chief among these are the subsystem of values, the political, economic, education, health, welfare, and communications subsystems. (Billingsley 1968, 5)

Hill, Billingsley, and others extended Billingsley's social systems approach to specify types of societal forces and social policies, community and family subsystems, and individual factors that affect the functioning of African American families. This approach can include both positive and negative factors and effects (Hill 1993).

## CAUSES AND CURES: MYTHS AND PROPOSITIONS

As we consider the influence of social factors and social forces it is helpful to dispense with two prominent arguments about the cause of the great increases in African American mother-only families—the "slavery-specific hypothesis" and the "welfare dependency argument."

### The "Black Matriarchy"

Several theories have been offered to explain the high rate of mother-only families among African Americans. One of the more prominent and persistent hypotheses was proposed nearly forty years ago by Daniel Patrick Moynihan, the future U.S. senator from New York. In 1965, Moynihan, then a U.S. Department of Labor official, described black families as "tangles of pathology" (Moynihan 1965, 29), which he stated was the result of a self-perpetuating matriarchal pattern of black family life. Blacks were forced into a matriarchal structure during slavery. In contrast to slavery in many other countries, there was no legal recognition of marriage among slaves in the United States. As a result, according to Moynihan, marriage was not a strong part of the culture of blacks during and after slavery. Rather, the black family tended to be matriarchal, with role reversal of husband and wife. Because this type of family structure was so out of line with the rest of American society, according to Moynihan, it retarded the progress of blacks as a group and led to what he termed the tangle of pathology.

Herbert Gutman (1976) discredited the slavery-specific hypothesis in his massive study of black families in slavery and in freedom between 1750 and 1925. He found that family was a strong cultural concept and practice throughout this period, and two-parent households and long-lasting marriages had been typical among African Americans for most of their American experience. He also demonstrated the fallacy in another of Moynihan's contentions: that family disorganization accompanied poor, southern black migrants to northern cities.

Therefore, the decline in African American two-parent families is not the result of some mystical cultural trend such as black matriarchy. It is the result of forces in the second half of the twentieth century, not slavery or age-old culture. If slavery was the causative factor, the proportion of mother-only African American households would have always been high. But, as shown in figure 7.1, two-parent families were the rule among African Americans until after 1960. For slavery to be the cause of current black fatherlessness, slavery's effect would have had to wait nearly one hundred years before it manifested itself. Marriage has been a prevalent trait in African American culture. At times, the marriage rate among African Americans has been higher than the rate for whites. Among women ages sixty-five years or older in 1973, only 4 percent of African Americans had never married, compared to 7 percent of whites (Burns and Scott 1994).

### The Welfare-Dependency Argument

Another popular theory on the cause of the increase in black mother-only families has been the availability of welfare payments (Murray 1984), but several scholars (Wilson 1987, Garfinkel and

**Figure 7.1 Percentage of U.S. Families with Two Parents, by Race, for Selected Years, 1890 to 1995**

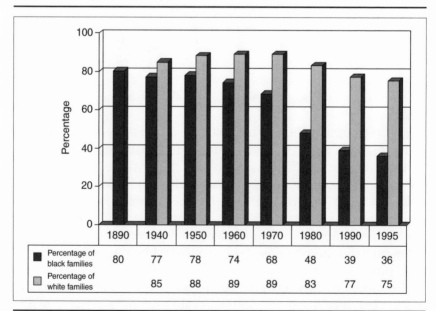

| | 1890 | 1940 | 1950 | 1960 | 1970 | 1980 | 1990 | 1995 |
|---|---|---|---|---|---|---|---|---|
| ■ Percentage of black families | 80 | 77 | 78 | 74 | 68 | 48 | 39 | 36 |
| ☐ Percentage of white families | | 85 | 88 | 89 | 89 | 83 | 77 | 75 |

*Source:* Authors' configuration based on U.S. Bureau of the Census (various years).

McLanahan 1989, Darity and Myers 1995) have shown this argument to be untenable.

## CAUSES AND CURES: HOLISTIC PERSPECTIVES

The holistic perspective in analyzing family structure and functioning as proposed by Hill (1993) requires the examination—or at least the consideration—of factors internal to the family and factors in the external community and the wider society. The decline in African American two-parent families is the result of multiple forces, the most important of which is the economic alienation of African American men. There is a strong correlation between black male employment and black female-headed families. As the black male unemployment rate increased between the mid-1960s and the 1990s, and as more black males dropped out of the labor force altogether (stopped looking for work), the percentage of black female-headed families rose correspondingly. Several scholars have demonstrated these relationships in elaborate detail (Wilson 1987; Lichter et al. 1992; Tucker and Mitchell-Kernan 1995). Darity and Myers (1995) showed that a combination of economic (black male employment) and demographic (sex ratios) factors was a better predictor of the percentage of female-headed families than sex ratios alone. Sampson (1995) showed that the causal effect of sex ratios on family structure among blacks is over five times greater than the sex-ratio effect on whites, and the male employment effect is twenty times greater on blacks than on whites.

## A BIG BEAR UPSTREAM: CRIMINALIZATION OF THE AFRICAN AMERICAN MALE

The traditional means of curing the economic alienation of African American men is through emphasis on education and job training. This undoubtedly should continue. However, an examination of relevant societal forces and social policies exposes another significant influence on the economic alienation of African American males: the operation of the criminal justice system.

One of the major reasons for the unavailability of African American men on the one hand and their economic alienation on the other hand is their overrepresentation in the criminal justice system. Although African Americans make up 12 percent of the U.S. population, they account for 28.1 percent of arrestees and over 50 percent of the yearly admissions to state and federal prisons (Garwood 1994).

Undoubtedly, much of this racial disparity is the result of two factors: the conditions in which many African American youth grow up and the differential treatment of African Americans at every phase of the criminal justice process (Reed et al. 1993). Differential treatment of African Americans is nowhere more evident than in the prosecution for illegal drug offenses. African Americans are 12 percent of the U.S. population and 13 percent of all drug users. Yet they account for 38 percent of all drug arrests, 59 percent of all drug convictions, and 74 percent of those sentenced to prison for drug offenses (Day 1995; Leadership Conference on Civil Rights 2001).

The situation is even more inequitable when one looks at convictions connected with crack cocaine. Consistently the majority of crack cocaine users are white, not black. The proportion of users who are black is less than 25 percent (U.S. Department of Health and Human Services 1996), yet 95 percent of all individuals incarcerated for crack cocaine are black. This disparate application of criminal justice sanctions to African Americans in general and African American males in particular is wreaking havoc on African American families and communities. Currently, on any given day, one-third of all African American men aged twenty to twenty-nine are under criminal justice supervision (Mauer and Huling 1995). These rates have reached epidemic proportions in some places. For example, in 1992, 42 percent of all the African American males aged eighteen to thirty-five who lived in the District of Columbia were in jail, in prison, on probation or parole, out on bond, or being sought on arrest warrants. In Baltimore the proportion was 56 percent. In the early 1990s one-sixth of black men sixteen years of age and older in the state of California were being arrested each year. African American males made up 3 percent of the state's population, yet they accounted for 40 percent of the state's inmates (Miller 1996).

The issue is not just incarceration, but the relationship between criminal conviction and employment. A criminal record has the effect of reducing employability when a felon leaves the criminal justice system (Freeman 1988). Thus, one scourge of African American communities, crime, is directly related to another perennial problem, unemployment.

## CONCLUSION

The holistic framework presented by Hill (1993) informs us of the multidimensional nature of factors that affect African American families. In this view the increasing rate of fatherlessness among black families is the result of multiple forces. Consequently, the prevention of fatherlessness requires several approaches. Using the public health model, I have argued that these approaches to preventing or intervening with fatherlessness should occur on all three levels—primary (prevention), secondary (prevention for at-risk population), and tertiary (remedial intervention).

Tertiary prevention, working with men who are absent fathers as well as their families, is necessary. There is a need to try to remedy the condition. There is also a need for secondary prevention, directed toward men who are at risk of becoming absent fathers. However, this work is like rescuing drowning individuals, especially at the tertiary level. We need to keep doing it, but we should also focus upstream: preventing men from falling or being put at risk of being pushed into the river.

As we focus upstream it is important to make more widely known the fact that some theories as to the cause of African American fatherlessness—black matriarchy and the welfare dependency—have been thoroughly discredited. The prevalence of these myths is influencing the direction of national attention to these issues, diverting attention and energy from more central factors.

More to the point is the economic alienation of African American men; this is undoubtedly the most important factor in the decreasing marriage rate among African Americans and consequently the increase in mother-only families. Although the debate may be ongoing about the causes of African American fatherlessness, it is clear that a man with a job is virtually a necessary, if not sufficient, condition for African American marriages.

An issue that is having increasing direct and indirect influence on African American fatherlessness is the growing criminalization of the African American male. With one-third of twenty- to twenty-nine-year-old African American men in the criminal justice system on any given day, African American families are seriously impacted. First, many of these men are fathers already, and those who are incarcerated are consequently absent fathers. In addition, these men will leave these institutions with criminal records, which will severely limit their employability and potential to be "marriageable males." This situation is bound to get worse in the near term if nothing is done to reverse the criminalization trend. This issue should be at the forefront of any "focusing upstream."

## REFERENCES

Angel, R. J., and J. L. Angel. 1993. *Painful Inheritance: Health and the New Generation of Fatherless Families*. Madison: University of Wisconsin Press.

Billingsley, Andrew. 1968. *Black Families in White America*. Englewood Cliffs, N.J.: Prentice-Hall.

Burns, Alisa, and Cathy Scott. 1994. *Mother-Headed Families and Why They Have Increased*. Hillsdale, N.J.: Lawrence Erlbaum.

Darity, W. A., and S. L. Myers Jr. 1995. "Family Structure and the Marginalization of Black Men: Policy Implications." In *The Decline in Marriage Among Africans: Causes, Consequences, and Policy Implications*, edited by Melinda B. Tucker and C. Mitchell-Kernan. New York: Russell Sage Foundation.

Dawson, D. A. 1991. "Family Structure and Children's Health and Well-Being: Data from the 1988 National Health Interview Survey on Child Health." *Journal of Marriage and the Family* 53(3): 573–84.

Day, Dawn. 1995. *Drug Arrests: Are Blacks Being Targeted?* Washington, D.C.: Sentencing Project.

Du Bois, W. E. B. 1898. "The Study of the Negro Problem." *Annals* 1(January):1–23.

———. 1967 [1899]. *The Philadelphia Negro: A Social Study*. New York: Schocken Books.

———. 1970 [1908]. *The Negro American Family*. Atlanta: Atlanta University Press. Cambridge, Mass.: MIT Press.

Freeman, R. B. 1988. "The Relation of Criminal Activity to Black Youth Employment." In *The Economics of Race and Crime*, edited by S. L. Myers, Jr., and M. C. Simms. New Brunswick, N.J.: Transaction Books.

Garfinkel, Irwin, and Sara McLanahan. 1989. *Single Mothers and Their Children: A New American Dilemma*. Washington, D.C.: Urban Institute Press.

Garwood, A. N., ed. 1994. *Black Americans: A Statistical Sourcebook*. Boulder, Colo.: Numbers and Concepts.

Gutman, H. G. 1976. *The Black Family in Slavery and Freedom, 1750–1925*. New York: Pantheon Books.

Hill, Robert. 1993. *Research on the African American Family: A Holistic Perspective*. Westport, Conn.: Auburn House Publishers.

Jaynes, G. D., and R. M. Williams. 1989. *A Common Destiny: Blacks and American Society*. Washington, D.C.: National Academy Press.

Leadership Conference on Civil Rights. 2001. *Justice on Trial: Racial Disparities in the Criminal Justice System*. Washington, D.C.: Leadership Conference on Civil Rights.

Lichter, D. T., D. K. McLaughlin, G. Kephart, and D. J. Landry. 1992. "Race and the Retreat from Marriage: A Shortage of Marriageable Men." *American Sociological Review* 57(6): 781–99.

Mauer, Marc, and Tracy Huling. 1995. *Intended and Unintended Consequences: State Racial Disparities in Imprisonment.* Washington, D.C.: Sentencing Project.

McLanahan, Sara, and Larry Bumpass. 1988. "Intergenerational Consequences of Family Disruption." *American Journal of Sociology* 94(1): 130–52.

McLanahan, Sara, and Gary D. Sandefur. 1994. *Growing Up with a Single Parent: What Hurts, What Helps.* Cambridge, Mass.: Harvard University Press.

Miller, J. G. 1996. *Search and Destroy: African-American Males in the Criminal Justice System.* New York: Cambridge University Press.

Moynihan, Daniel P. 1965. *The Negro Family: The Case for National Action.* Washington: Office of Policy Planning and Research, United States Department of Labor.

Murray, Charles. 1984. *Losing Ground: American Social Policy, 1950–1980.* New York: Basic Books.

Parsons, Talcott. 1951. *The Social System.* New York: Free Press.

Parsons, Talcott, and R. F. Bales. 1955. *Family, Socialization and Interaction Process.* New York: Free Press.

Reed, W. L., et al. 1993. "The Administration of Justice." In *African Americans: Essential Perspectives,* edited by Wornie Reed. Westport, Conn.: Auburn House.

Sampson, Robert J. 1995. "Unemployment and Imbalanced Sex Ratios: Race-Specific Consequences for Family Structure and Crime." In *The Decline in Marriage Among African Americans: Causes, Consequences, and Policy Implications,* edited by M. B. Tucker and C. Mitchell-Kernan. New York: Russell Sage Foundation.

Tucker, Melinda B., and C. Mitchell-Kernan, eds. 1995. *The Decline in Marriage Among African Americans: Causes, Consequences, and Policy Implications.* New York: Russell Sage Foundation.

U.S. Department of Health and Human Services. 1996. *National Household Survey on Drug Abuse: Population Estimates, 1995.* Rockville, Md.: U.S. Department of Health and Human Services, Public Health Service, Alcohol, Drug Abuse, and Mental Health Administration.

Wilson, William J. 1987. *The Truly Disadvantaged: The Inner City, The Underclass, and Public Policy.* Chicago: University of Chicago Press.

Zill, N., and C. A. Schoenborn. 1990. "Developmental, Learning, and Emotional Problems: Health of our Nation's Children, United States, 1988." *Advance Data from Vital and Health Statistics,* no. 190. Hyattsville, Md.: National Center for Health Statistics.

# Chapter 8

## IS IT WORKING? EARLY EVALUATIONS OF FATHERHOOD-RENEWAL PROGRAMS

### WADE F. HORN

There is a new consensus that fathers matter to the well-being of their children. Research consistently finds that, even after income and other sociodemographic variables have been controlled for, children who grow up with the active involvement of a responsible father are less likely to fail at school, develop behavioral and emotional problems, get into trouble with the law, engage in early and promiscuous sexual activity, or become welfare-dependent later in life than those who do not have such a father (for a review of this literature see Horn 1999). The question no longer is whether father involvement matters, but what we can do to encourage more of it.

One consequence of this new consensus has been a veritable explosion over the past decade of community-based organizations offering support, outreach, and skills training to fathers. Indeed, in March of 1994, when I participated in launching the National Fatherhood Initiative, the organization could barely locate two hundred operational fatherhood programs in the United States. Today, it is estimated that there are well over two thousand such programs nationwide. Although different fatherhood interventions target different populations, most programs working with African Americans have thus far focused on low-income noncustodial fathers.

How effective are these new fatherhood programs, especially those that target African American fathers? In particular, to what extent are fatherhood interventions aimed at low-income noncustodial African American fathers successful at increasing work effort and employment level, improving child-support payment rates, increasing father-child involvement, and, most important, enhancing child well-being?

Unfortunately, answers to these important questions are limited by the fact that to date, there have been very few evaluations of the effectiveness of fatherhood programs. The studies that have been completed have mostly been descriptive in nature and process-oriented. Few have focused on outcomes. Those that have focused on outcomes rarely have included random assignment of subjects to program and control groups, the sine qua non of a good evaluation study. Most disappointing of all, the few evaluations that have been undertaken have yielded mixed results at best.

Nevertheless, studies of the effectiveness of fatherhood interventions are extremely important, not only as a means for determining the impact of current efforts, but also for enhancing the effectiveness of future interventions. This chapter will review what we know about the effectiveness of fatherhood programs working with low-income and mostly noncustodial fathers.

## RESULTS OF NONEXPERIMENTAL EVALUATIONS OF FATHERHOOD PROGRAMS

Thus far, most evaluations of the effectiveness of fatherhood interventions with African Americans have focused on programs working with low-income noncustodial fathers. Consequently, the major dependent variables of interest have been earnings, child-support payment rates, and satisfaction with fatherhood peer support groups. Regrettably, virtually no attention has been focused in these early evaluations on improvements in child well-being, the presumed ultimate outcome of interest.

One problem commonly reported in these evaluations is difficulty recruiting and maintaining the participation of low-income fathers. For example, in an evaluation of the Parent Opportunity Project (POP), initiated by the Denver Division of Child Support Enforcement to help low-income fathers get jobs, pay child support, and become more involved with their children, only a third of the fathers recruited for the program eventually participated, and those who did frequently failed to follow through with the recommendations of the program (Pearson and Thoennes 1999, 1). Recruitment was also found to be a "major issue" in a multisite evaluation of responsible-fatherhood projects funded by the U.S. Department of Health and Human Services, causing these projects to be implemented "more slowly than originally planned" (Price 1999, 3–4).

One reason for difficulty recruiting fathers is suspicion concerning the program's true objectives, especially when the program has official ties with child-support enforcement. Indeed, an early process evaluation of a fatherhood program in San Mateo County, California, found that many dads thought that because the program was operated by the attorney general's office, which houses the office of child-support enforcement, it was really a "sting" operation (Price 1999, A9).

Another reason for difficulty in recruiting fathers is that frequently the primary source for locating the father is the mother. Unless the mother has an ongoing and positive relationship with the father, she is often unwilling or unable to provide information as to the father's whereabouts. Even if the mother has a positive relationship with the father, she may be reluctant to provide contact information if she fears doing so will lead to his arrest for nonpayment of child support or other criminal infractions. Indeed, an early process evaluation of the Baltimore City Healthy Start Men's Services Program found that only half of the mothers contacted were willing or able to provide information concerning the father's whereabouts (Barnow et al. 1997, B9).

Despite these recruitment difficulties, fathers who do participate generally report high levels of satisfaction with the program, and especially the fatherhood peer support groups. For instance, participants in Denver's POP program reported a high level of satisfaction with the program and credited it with helping them to parent, visit with their children, and feel hopeful about the future. Unfortunately, satisfaction with the program does not necessarily correlate with improved outcomes on other measures. Despite a great deal of satisfaction with the POP program, there was no change in either employment rates or payment of child support obligations as a consequence of participation in the program.

One notable exception to these otherwise disappointing results is an evaluation of a Cleveland-based program administered by the Institute for Responsible Fatherhood and Family Revitalization (IRFFR). The primary goal of the IRFFR is to reconnect fathers with their children. The underlying philosophy of the program is that reconnecting fathers with their children will lead to positive changes in both attitudes and behavior, including increased employment, establishment of paternity, payment of child support, and father involvement. The primary service is in-home counseling provided by outreach specialists, frequently a married couple, who are required to live in the community serviced by the program.

An independent evaluation of 151 clients, primarily young fathers between fifteen and twenty-five years of age, found that 97 percent of the participants agreed that the program helped them feel better about themselves, 97 percent agreed that the program had taught them to be a responsible parent, and 92 percent agreed that the program had encouraged them to complete their education. Even more impressive, 70 percent of the clients, called protégés by the IRFFR, reported providing financial support for three or more persons (including themselves); 97 percent agreed that the program had helped them to provide psychological and emotional support for their children; 97 percent agreed that the program influenced them to spend more time with their children; and 96 percent agreed that the program helped them create a better environment for their children to grow and develop (Nixon and King 1994). Unfortunately, the lack of a randomly assigned control group and outcome measures independent of the protégés themselves limits the usefulness of this evaluation.

## RESULTS OF THE EXPERIMENTAL EVALUATIONS OF FATHERHOOD PROGRAMS

Only three evaluations of fatherhood-promotion programs could be located that incorporated a randomized, experimental design and multiple outcome measures. As was the case with nonexperimental evaluations of fatherhood programs, these three experimental evaluation studies focused on programs for low-income noncustodial fathers that were designed to enhance employment, payment of child support, and father involvement. Unfortunately, the results of these experimental evaluations are no more encouraging than those employing nonexperimental designs, and in some cases they are even less so.

The first of these studies is an evaluation of the Children First program operated by Goodwill Industries of Southeastern Wisconsin (Barnow et al. 1997, appendix D, 1–9). The Children First program, begun in 1990, is conducted in cooperation with the Racine, Wisconsin, County Human Services Department and the county Child Support Enforcement Agency. The goals of the program are to identify noncustodial fathers and reconnect them with their children; enhance the fathers' ability to provide financially for their children through employment activities; and increase the level and consistency of child-support payments.

A small number of fathers who had been identified for enrollment in Children First were randomly assigned to a control group (n = 103). The control group received the same type of services—primarily court-ordered job search—that they would have received without participating in the Children First program. Program participants received individualized case management, employment services, and training in father responsibility and parenting skills.

Fathers in the control group actually paid *more* in child support at both six and twelve months following referral to the program or control group (at twelve months, $466 versus $375 per month). Control-group fathers also made a greater number of child-support payments than program participants at both six and twelve months after referral to the program or control group (at twelve months, 6.46 versus 5.71).

A second study employing random assignment and multiple outcome measures was an evaluation of eight geographically diverse federally funded demonstration projects designed to resolve problems related to noncustodial parents' access to their children through mediation, parent education, counseling, and telephone monitoring (Pearson et al. 1996). The goal of the evaluation was to assess the extent to which the intervention successfully decreased the amount of time required to resolve access disputes, reduced litigation related to access disputes, improved compliance with court-ordered child-support payments, and promoted the adjustment of children. Unfortunately, the evaluation report does not provide information on either the socioeconomic or racial composition of the program participants. Nevertheless, the results of this evaluation are reviewed here because of its emphasis on enhancing noncustodial-parent (mostly fathers) involvement with their children and improving child outcomes.

As discussed earlier, recruitment is a challenge for fatherhood interventions in general. Consistent with this pattern, attendance at mediation sessions was a substantial problem. The percentage of parents who were assigned to mediation but failed to appear ranged from 7 to 94 percent of the cases, depending upon the demonstration site. Moreover, there was little evidence that the mediation intervention resulted for the noncustodial parent in either enhanced access to the child or increased contact with the child. Furthermore, although child-support compliance rates did increase in some sites, at the follow-up stage of the study, no differences were found in parental ratings of children's problem behaviors between those who had received services and those who had not.

By far the most comprehensive and best-designed evaluation of a fatherhood promotion program is the evaluation by the Manpower Demonstration and Research Corporation (MDRC) of the multi-site Parents' Fair Share program (Doolittle et al. 1998; Johnson and Doolittle 1996). The Parents' Fair Share Demonstration was designed to help noncustodial fathers who owed child support to find more stable and better-paying jobs, pay child support on a consistent basis, and assume a fuller and more responsible fathering role. Key services included peer support, employment and training services, and voluntary mediation between custodial and noncustodial parents.

In exchange for participation in the program, the noncustodial fathers were given "breathing room" from their child-support obligations by means of a temporary lowering of the amount they were required to pay. Once a noncustodial father found employment, however, his child-support obligations were raised to an appropriate level. If a noncustodial father ceased to participate in the program, child-support payment enforcement staff were instructed to quickly enforce the preprogram level of child-support obligations. Noncustodial fathers who met the program eligibility criteria were randomly assigned to the program or to a control group subject to normal child-support payment enforcement procedures.

The overall sample—those in the program group and in the control group—consisted of 2,641 noncustodial fathers in seven cities: Dayton, Ohio; Grand Rapids, Michigan; Jacksonville, Florida; Los Angeles, California; Memphis, Tennessee; Springfield, Illinois; and Trenton, New Jersey. About eighty percent of this sample of fathers were African American or Hispanic; only 40 percent had ever been married (although not necessarily to the mother of the child who was the focus of Parents' Fair Share services); most were unemployed (43 percent had earned a total of $500 or less in the three quarters prior to their entry into the program); 20 percent had paid some child support in the quarter prior to enrollment in the program; and all had substantial child-support arrears.

The evaluation found that two years after program implementation, Parents' Fair Share produced some modest increases in employment and earnings among the most disadvantaged subset of fathers, but there was no impact for the sample as a whole (Knox and Redcross 2000). In addition, although Parents' Fair Share participants were more likely to pay formal child support through the child support enforcement system than those in the control group (50 percent versus 43 percent) and paid significantly higher amounts ($397 per quarter versus $313), the study also found that pressuring these fathers to provide more support through the formal child-support payment enforcement system resulted in reduced levels of informal support (that is, cash or in-kind support provided directly to the custodial parent).

Regarding noneconomic aspects of father involvement, Parents' Fair Share reported that the noncustodial fathers did seem to genuinely care about and want to be involved with their children. Moreover, fathers in the program reported finding the peer support groups, designed to teach effective fathering skills, helpful. The program did not, however, significantly increase the amount of time noncustodial fathers spent with their children, although it did produce some increase in father-child contact in families with very low levels of initial visitation. Regrettably, no data have yet been made available as to whether or not participation in the peer support groups resulted in improved child well-being.

## LESSONS LEARNED

There are a number of important lessons to be learned from these evaluations, though the lessons are somewhat disappointing.

*Lesson 1: Promoting responsible fatherhood is hard work.* Prior research suggests that low-income unwed fathers are unlikely to pay child support or stay connected to their children over the long term. The hope of the Parents' Fair Share project was that peer support, employment, and mediation services would enhance the likelihood that low-income, unwed fathers would become and stay involved in their children's lives, both financially and emotionally, and in so doing would improve the well-being of their children. Apparently not even this level of services is adequate to the task.

The finding that this is hard work should come as no surprise. It is only recently that the importance of fatherhood, and especially the noneconomic aspects of fatherhood, has come back into fashion in popular and policy discussions. It is naive to think that a single program will yield strong effects on positive father involvement if that program operates within a broader cultural context that still regularly and consistently provides negative messages about the importance of father involvement to the well-being of children. This suggests that community-based fatherhood programs cannot be content with delivering services to individual clients. They must also be actively involved in, or at least supportive of, efforts to change the broader social-cultural understanding of fatherhood as an institution and its importance to children, families, and communities.

*Lesson 2: Father-involvement services and child-support enforcement may not mix easily.* Many fatherhood programs targeted to African Americans and focusing on working with low-income, noncustodial fathers, have been designed to work in conjunction with efforts to enforce child support. This may be a mistake. There may simply be too many negative associations with child-support enforcement on the part of low-income noncustodial fathers to make this partnership tenable. Moreover, too great a focus on the payment of child support can mean that the many noneconomic contributions that fathers make to the well-being of their children end up being ignored. The fact that the formal child-support system often dismisses the informal support that low-income noncustodial fathers sometimes provide their children may lead many of these men to conclude the only thing the formal system is interested in is their money.

If fathers are to be more than cash machines for their children, fatherhood programs will need to emphasize and support their contribution as nurturers, disciplinarians, mentors, moral instructors, and skill coaches, and not just as economic providers. Doing otherwise is to downgrade fathers to "paper fatherhood," in the words of Barbara Dafoe Whitehead (Whitehead 1998, 171).

This does not mean that child-support payment enforcement is unimportant. Any man who fathers a child outside of wedlock ought to be held responsible for helping to ensure the financial viability of that child. Indeed, research generally substantiates that child well-being is improved when nonresident fathers pay child support (for a review of this literature see Garfinkel et al. 1998). In addition, during the 1990s, many state and local child-support agencies began working to expand the mission of the formal child-support system to include helping noncustodial parents fulfill their noneconomic responsibilities as well as their economic ones. Despite these efforts, the results of the Parents' Fair Share evaluation and others suggest that, at least in the near term, the most effective father-involvement programs may be those that operate relatively independent of the formal child-support enforcement system.

*Lesson 3: Fatherhood programs need to intervene earlier.* By working with low-income noncustodial fathers who are already behind on their child support, Parents' Fair Share, and other fatherhood programs like it, may be intervening too late. By then, many noncustodial, unwed fathers may already have become disconnected from their children and alienated from the child's mother, or may have moved on to other partners. Indeed, in a national study following 13,000 youth ages fourteen to twenty-one, Robert Lerman and Theodora Ooms (1993) found that 57 percent of unwed fathers with children no older than two years of age visited their children more than once per week, whereas only 23 percent who had children seven and a half or older were in frequent contact with their children.

These data suggest that fatherhood programs may be more effective if the point of intervention is very early, while the mother is pregnant or shortly after the child's birth. That way, the fatherhood program will be intervening while the couple's relationship is still reasonably strong and before child-support arrears have built up. In fact, recent data from the Fragile Families Initiative indicate that at the time of an out-of-wedlock birth, 82 percent of low-income couples are romantically involved, 53 percent are cohabiting, and 86 percent of the fathers have plans to help with the child in the future. Only 6 percent of the mothers reported at the time of the child's birth they did not want the father to be involved with the child.

Fatherhood programs may be more successful at encouraging positive father involvement by intervening at this early stage in this fragile family's life, when the father's relationship with both his child and the mother may be more readily strengthened and solidified. Anecdotal evidence from programs such as the Healthy Start Men's Services Program in Baltimore, as well as the Institute for Responsible Fatherhood and Family Revitalization (IRFFR), seem to confirm this hope. To date, however, no systematic evaluations employing random assignment to intervention and control groups have been undertaken to test this proposition.

*Lesson 4: Programs that focus on increasing visitation for low-income fathers may not be enough to improve child well-being.* Most studies have not found frequency of visitation by nonresident fathers to be consistently associated with improvements in child outcomes. Improvements are dependent on the type of activities and interactions fathers have with their children. Research has found that children whose nonresident fathers engage in authoritative parenting—listening to their problems, giving them advice, providing explanations for rules, monitoring their academic performance, helping with their homework, engaging in mutual projects, and disciplining them—are significantly more likely to do well at school and to evidence greater psychological health than children whose fathers mostly engage them in recreational activities, such as going out to dinner, taking them on vacations, and buying them things (Amato and Gilbreth 1999, 557–73). Hence, the right type of involvement of nonresidential fathers can have a positive impact on child well-being.

Unfortunately, other research indicates that nonresident fathers are unlikely to engage in authoritative parenting, especially when compared with in-the-home fathers (Hetherington 1993, 39–46; see also Furstenberg and Nord 1985, 893–904). One reason for this is constraints inherent in traditional visitation arrangements. Because their time with their children is often severely limited, many nonresident fathers strive to make sure their children enjoy themselves when they are with them. As a result, nonresident fathers tend to spend less time than in-the-home fathers helping their children with their homework, monitoring their activities, and setting appropriate limits and more time taking them to restaurants or the movies, activities that have not been found to be associated with enhanced child outcomes. Thus, although visitation by nonresident fathers is certainly something to be encouraged, the context of visitation makes it unlikely that nonresident fathers will actually engage in the kinds of behaviors associated with improvements in child well-being.

*Lesson 5: Strengthening cohabitation may not be sufficient for improving child well-being either.* Recently, some fatherhood programs have begun to focus on strengthening cohabiting relationships. But cohabitation is unlikely to deliver a lifetime father to children. That's because cohabitation is a very weak family form, especially in comparison to legal marriage. Cohabiting couples break up at much higher rates than do married couples, and although 40 to 50 percent of couples who have a child while cohabiting go on to get married, they are more likely to divorce than couples who get married before having children (Moore 1995, vii). Overall, three-quarters of children born to cohabiting parents will see their parents split up before they reach age sixteen, compared to only about one-third of children born to married parents (Popenoe and Whitehead 1999, 7).

Once a father no longer lives with his children, his involvement with his children declines rapidly (King 1994, 78–96; see also Seltzer 1991, 79–101). Indeed, 40 percent of children in father-absent homes have not seen their father in over a year. Of the remaining 60 percent, only one in five sleeps even one night per month in the father's home. Overall, only one in six children with fathers living away from home sees her or his father once a week or more, on average (Furstenberg and Nord 1985, 896).

The fact is that children born to cohabiting couples are likely to see their fathers become occasional visitors before too long. Extrapolating from the research literature on attachment theory (Bowlby 1969), it may be that child outcomes are actually *worse* for children whose fathers are involved early on, but then disappear, compared to those whose fathers are continuously absent. If so, focusing on strengthening cohabitation may actually be making a bad situation worse.

Moreover, many men in cohabiting relationships are not the biological father of the children in the household, or at least are not the biological father of all the children in the household. By one estimate, 63 percent of children in cohabiting households are born not to the cohabiting couple but to a previous union of one of the adult partners, most often the mother (Graefe and Lichter 1999). This is problematic in that there is substantial evidence indicating that cohabitation with a man who is not biologically related to the children increases substantially the risk of both physical and sexual child abuse (Whelan 1993, 29, table 12; see also Daly and Wilson 1996; Margolin 1992, 541–51). Thus, not only is cohabitation unlikely to deliver a long-term father to a child, but if the man is cohabiting with another man's children, those children are placed at an increased risk for child abuse. Unfortunately, most fatherhood programs have largely ignored this issue.

*Lesson 6: Fatherhood programs need to begin talking about marriage.* Most fatherhood programs for low-income noncustodial fathers focus on helping them find jobs, pay child support, and visit or cohabit with their children. Few fatherhood programs discuss the topic of marriage. Many exclude married fathers from participation altogether. This model may be inadequate to the task of delivering the one thing that children want and need most: an involved, committed, and responsible father. By steadfastly avoiding the topic of marriage or, worse still, restricting participation in the program to men who have fathered a child out of wedlock, fatherhood programs may be communicating the idea that marriage doesn't matter to fatherhood.

The empirical evidence suggests otherwise. Married fathers are far more likely to have a close and enduring relationship with their children and to exert a positive influence on them than unmarried fathers.

The empirical evidence also is quite clear that adults—women as well as men—are happier, healthier, and wealthier than their single counterparts (Stack and Eshleman 1998, 527–36; see also Gallagher 1996; Waite 1995, 483–507). By avoiding discussions about the importance of marriage to fatherhood, we may be losing the opportunity both to prevent unwed fathers from fathering additional children out of wedlock (and thereby further reducing their ability to fulfill their responsibilities as fathers) and to communicate the ideal of married fatherhood to the next generation of fathers.

This is not to say that efforts to reach out to low-income unwed fathers should be abandoned. Children want and need their father, whether their father is married or not. We do not have a father to spare. Nevertheless, fatherhood programs should broaden their target population to provide outreach, support, and skills building not only to noncustodial fathers but also to married fathers. Otherwise, fatherhood programs run the risk of instituting perverse incentives for fathering children out of wedlock, in much the same way welfare has historically provided perverse incentives for women to bear children out of wedlock. Indeed, some programs aggressively advertise unique benefits, such as state-of-the-art physical fitness facilities, to inner-city low-income men so long as they do one thing—father a child out of wedlock. Although programs may not intend to do so, restricting such benefits to unwed fathers amounts to rewarding out-of-wedlock fathering. This is hardly a message likely to reinforce the value of marriage.

Some will object to the idea of incorporating a strong pro-marriage message into fatherhood programs, believing that to do so ignores the problem of domestic violence and is tantamount to imposing middle-class, majority-culture values on reluctant lower-income minority communities. But the available evidence suggests otherwise. To be sure, some married households are horrible places for both children and adults, but nevertheless, the reality is that domestic violence and child abuse are substantially *less* likely to occur in intact, married households than in any other family arrangements. Furthermore, promoting marriage as the ideal does not mean programs should ignore issues of domestic violence. To the contrary, promoting healthy marriages requires that programs first assess the potential for violence in the couple's relationship.

In regard to the desirability of marriage, research by Sarah McLanahan and Irv Garfinkel (2000) found that two-thirds of low-income, unwed couples at the time of their child's birth want—and expect—to get married. It is not a question, therefore, of imposing middle-class "marriage values" on reluctant low-income couples, but of helping low-income couples achieve something they say they want for themselves—lasting, stable marriages.

## CONCLUSION

Evaluations of social programs are bound to disappoint. As Peter Rossi, a noted program evaluator, has pointed out in his "Iron Law of Evaluation" "the expected value of any net impact assessment of any large scale social program is zero." His "Stainless Steel Law of Evaluation" states that "the better designed the impact assessment of a social program, the more likely is the resulting impact of net impact to be zero" (Rossi 1987, 4). Thus we should not be too discouraged when some evaluations of fatherhood programs show less than satisfying results. Instead, we should seize upon the results of negative evaluations to better understand what *doesn't* work. If we fail to learn those lessons we run the risk not only of wasting precious resources on ineffective programs but also of missing an opportunity offered by the current public interest in doing something about the crisis of fatherlessness.

---

The views expressed in this chapter do not necessarily represent the views of the Administration for Children and Families, the U.S. Department of Health and Human Services, or the United States Government.

## REFERENCES

Amato, Paul, and Joan G. Gilbreth. 1999. "Non-Resident Fathers and Children's Well-Being: A Meta-Analysis." *Journal of Marriage and the Family* 61(August): 557–73.

Barnow, Burt S., David C. Stapleton, Gina Livermore, Jeffrey Johnson, and John Trukto. 1997. *An Evaluability Assessment of Responsible Fatherhood Programs: Final Report.* Washington, D.C.: The Lewin Group, Inc.

Bowlby, John. 1969. *Attachment.* New York: Basic Books.

Daly, Martin, and Margo Wilson. 1996. "Evolutionary Psychology and Marital Conflict: The Relevance of Stepchildren." In *Sex, Power, Conflict: Evolutionary and Feminist Perspectives,* edited by David M. Buss and Neil Malamuth. New York: Oxford University Press.

Doolittle, Fred, Virginia Knox, Cynthia Miller, and Sharon Rowser. 1998. *Building Opportunities, Enforcing Obligations: Implementation and Interim Impacts of Parents' Fair Share.* New York: Manpower Demonstration Research Corporation.

Furstenberg, Frank F., and Christine Winquiest Nord. 1985. "Parenting Apart: Patterns of Child Rearing After Marital Disruption." *Journal of Marriage and the Family* 47(November): 893–904.

Gallagher, Maggie. 1996. *The Abolition of Marriage.* Washington, D.C.: Regnery.

Garfinkel, Irwin, Sara S. McLanahan, Daniel R. Meyer, and Judith A. Seltzer, eds. 1998. *Fathers Under Fire: The Revolution in Child Support Enforcement.* New York: Russell Sage Foundation.

Graefe, Deborah R., and Daniel T. Lichter. 1999. "Life Course Transitions of American Children: Parental Cohabitation, Marriage, and Single Motherhood." *Demography* 36(May): 205–17.

Heatherington, E. Mavis. 1993. "An Overview of the Virginia Longitudinal Study of Divorce and Remarriage with a Focus on Early Adolescence." *Journal of Family Psychology* 7(June): 39–56.

Horn, Wade F. 1999. *Father Facts.* 3rd ed. Gaithersburg, Md.: National Fatherhood Initiative.

Johnson, Earl S., and Fred Doolittle. 1996. *Low-Income Parents and the Parents' Fair Share Demonstration: An Early Qualitative Look at Low-Income Non-custodial Parents (NCPS) and How One Policy Initiative Has Attempted to Improve their Ability to Pay Child Support.* New York: Manpower Demonstration Research Corporation

King, V. 1994. "Non-Resident Father Involvement and Child Well-Being." *Journal of Family Issues* 15(March): 78–96.

Knox, Virginia, and Cindy Red Cross. 2000. "Parenting and Providing: The Impact of Parents' Fair Share on Paternal Involvement." Report. New York: Manpower Demonstration Research Corporation.

Lerman, Robert, and Theodora Ooms, eds. 1993. *Young, Unwed Fathers: Changing Roles and Emerging Policies.* Philadelphia: Temple University Press.

Margolin, Leslie. 1992. "Child Abuse by Mothers' Boyfriends: Why the Over-Representation?" *Child Abuse and Neglect* 16(July-August): 541–51.

McLanahan, Sarah, and Irv Garfinkel. 2000. "Dispelling Myths About Unmarried Fathers." Fragile Families Research Brief 1 (May), Bendheim-Thoman Center for Research on Child Well-Being, Princeton University, and Social Indicators Survey Center, Columbia University.

McManus, Michael J. 1995. *Marriage Savers: Helping Your Friends and Family Avoid Divorce.* Grand Rapids, Mich.: Zondervan Publishing House.

Moore, Kristin A. 1995. "Nonmarital Childbearing in the United States." Report to Congress on out-of-wedlock childbearing. Washington: U.S. Department of Health and Human Services.

Nixon, G. Regina, and Anthony E. O. King. 1994. *Former Protégé (Client) Outcome Survey (1982–1992)*. Cleveland: Institute for Responsible Fatherhood and Family Revitalization.

Pearson, Jessica, and Nancy Thoennes. 1999. *An Evaluation of the Parent Opportunity Project*. Denver, Colo.: Center for Policy Research.

Pearson, Jessica, Nancy Thoennes, David Price, and Robert Williams. 1996. *Evaluations of the Child Access Demonstration Projects: Report to Congress*. Denver, Colo.: Center for Policy Research and Policy Studies, Inc.

Popenoe, David, and Barbara Dafoe Whitehead. 1999. *Should We Live Together? What Young Adults Need to Know About Cohabitation Before Marriage*. New Brunswick, N.J.: National Marriage Project.

Price, David. 1999. *Multisite Evaluation and Synthesis of Responsible Fatherhood Projects, Quarterly Progress Report: 4/1/99–6/30/99*. Denver, Colo.: Policy Studies, Inc.

Rossi, Peter H. 1987. "The Iron Law of Evaluation and Other Metallic Rules." *Research in Social Problems and Public Policy* 4: 3–20.

Seltzer, J. A. 1991. "Relationships Between Fathers and Children Who Live Apart: The Father's Role After Separation." *Journal of Marriage and the Family* 53(February): 79–101.

Stack, Steven, and J. Ross Eshleman. 1998. "Marital Status and Happiness: A 17-Nation Study." *Journal of Marriage and the Family* 60(May): 527–36.

Waite, Linda J. 1995. "Does Marriage Matter?" *Demography* 32(November): 483–507.

Whelan, Robert. 1993. *Broken Homes and Battered Children: A Study of the Relationship Between Child Abuse and Family Type*. London: Family Education Trust.

Whitehead, Barbara Dafoe. 1998. *The Divorce Culture: Rethinking Our Commitments to Marriage and Family*. New York: Vintage Books.

# Chapter 9

## MAKING THE WOUNDED WHOLE: MARRIAGE AS CIVIL RIGHT AND CIVIC RESPONSIBILITY

### ENOLA G. AIRD

Item 1: Two young black girls are playing. One says to the other, "Let's play house." The second responds, "Sure, you be the mommy, I'll be the day-care center."

Item 2: An African American teenage boy appears before a probation officer for an initial interview. The boy is asked a series of questions about his mother. He answers with absolute confidence. When asked about his father, he is able to give a name and a few details, but answers most of the questions with pain in his eyes, saying, "I really don't know."

Item 3: A young African American man on a ride home after an event at a youth center says—out of the blue—to one of the adult leaders, "Women are better than men." Stunned, the adult responds, "Why do you say that?" "Because," says the young man, "at least women stay with their children."

These are true stories about children I know—four of the real children behind one of the most alarming statistics about the African American community: In spite of some recent encouraging news as noted by the editors of this volume, the fact is that a majority of African American children are born to unmarried mothers and fathers. These stories are illustrative of one of the major challenges confronting the black community.

In the late 1940s and early 1950s, the psychologist Kenneth Clark and his colleagues amassed considerable evidence demonstrating that black children were being harmed by this country's system of segregated schools. Their work helped to drive a far-reaching civil rights movement that led ultimately to desegregation in education and in many other areas of American life.

Today, half a century later, there is a compelling and growing body of evidence showing that the problem of unwed parenting is causing profound harm to black children. The evidence of harm is as strong as or stronger than the evidence gathered by Kenneth Clark and his associates to justify the massive civil rights mobilizations of the last century.

## THE EVIDENCE OF HARM TO OUR CHILDREN

Across the United States, a large number of women and men are having children without committing themselves to each other and to their children through the institution of marriage. The proportion of births that are out of wedlock has risen dramatically for all races and ethnic groups since 1970 and the proportion of children living with only one parent has more than doubled over the same period (Ooms 1998, 46). Although the recent rate of increase in out-of-wedlock births has been the fastest for whites (and the rise in the proportion of children living with only one parent has been the steepest for whites), the proportions have been the highest for African Americans (Ooms 1998, 46).

On this matter as in so many others, the old adage holds: when white America catches a cold, black America catches pneumonia. The crisis of declining marriage rates and the rise in the number of households headed by single mothers has affected all races, ethnic groups, and classes in the United States. But it has been especially acute for African Americans, with devastating consequences for black children.

At least 80 percent of all African American children will spend a significant part of their childhood years living apart from their fathers (Morehouse Research Institute and Institute for American Values 1999, 4). A growing number of black children live in neighborhoods that are "radically fatherless," that is, they live in homes headed by single mothers in neighborhoods in which more than 50 percent of all families with children are headed by single mothers. In 1990, approximately 4.5 million children lived in such neighborhoods, and of these children, nearly 80 percent were African Americans (Morehouse Research Institute 1999, 8).

Even in the best of circumstances, the work of raising black children in the United States is extremely challenging. We can ill afford to compound that challenge. But for the majority of black children born today, the challenge is being exacerbated by the circumstances of their birth and the structure of the families in which they are being raised. The data clearly show that one family form is not as good as another. On average, children raised by single parents do not fare as well as children raised by their two married parents. A growing body of research, carefully controlled for a wide variety of variables, including race, income, housing location, and other factors, is showing that father absence, in and of itself, is a major cause of negative outcomes in children's lives (Coalition for Marriage, Family and Couples Education 2000, 8). When compared to children living with their married parents, children who do not live with their fathers are five times as likely to be poor. They are less likely to perform well in high school and are twice as likely to be high school dropouts (McLanahan and Sandefur 1994, 1). Boys and young men brought up in single-parent homes are two times as likely, and boys raised in stepfamilies are three times as likely, to commit a crime that leads to imprisonment (Harper and McLanahan 1998). A child growing up with only one parent is at greater risk of being a victim of a crime, especially child abuse (Daly and Wilson 1996, 9–28).

According to the researchers Sara McLanahan and Gary Sandefur (1994, 1) who conducted a major study of differences between children raised by single parents and children raised by two married parents, "Children who grow up in a household with only one biological parent are worse off, on average, than children who grow up in a household with both their biological parents, regardless of the parents' race or educational background, regardless of whether the resident parent remarries." In their book, *The Case for Marriage*, Linda Waite and Maggie Gallagher (2000, 125) sum up the evidence: children raised in single-parent households are, on average, more likely to be poor, to have health problems and psychological disorders, to commit crimes and exhibit other conduct disorders, have somewhat poorer relationships with both family and peers, and as adults eventually get fewer years of education and enjoy less stable marriages and lower occupational status on average than children whose parents got and stayed married. This "marriage gap" in children's well-being remains in force even after researchers control for important family characteristics, including parents' race, income, and socioeconomic status.

The most compelling evidence that unwed parenting and father absence is causing harm to our children is found in the testimony of children themselves, like that of the children described at the beginning of this paper. These are children I know by name. I have known them for over five years. They live in a public housing development in an urban neighborhood in which fathers are absent entirely or are transitory figures at best. Without a critical mass of fathers and husbands in the neighborhood, young boys hang out on street corners trying to figure out for themselves what it means to be a man. I can attest, as the urban anthropologist Elijah Anderson (1999) has observed, that in the absence of strong male role models, these young men design for themselves elaborate codes of manhood, codes that are often self-defeating, self-destructive, and violent. The young girls of the neighborhood, growing up without the consistent presence of their fathers, often lack a sense of their own self-worth and frequently end up in relationships that are self-defeating, self-destructive, and painful. In their search for love and affirmation, many of these young men and women often enter into fleeting sexual relationships that bring new fragile human beings into the world on the same shaky, often painful, family foundations on which their young mothers and fathers grew up.

Kevin Powell (1997), author of *Keepin' It Real*, in an open letter to his father, describes in moving terms the "unbearable pain" of unwed parenting and father absence: "My mother and you never being married messed me up something awful," he says. He uses bell hooks's term "inwardly homeless" to describe his feelings of abandonment: "The worst thing a child can feel is that he doesn't have a true home, a place where he feels nurtured in a way that confirms his life. I mean, if he can't trust his own parents, really, whom can he trust? Whom can that child love if he feels he has never been loved by the very people who brought him into the world?" (Powell 1997, 81–83)

Too many African American children are growing up weighed down by the "unbearable pain" that comes with knowing that the people who brought them into the world could not stay together for the sake of their children. Too many of our children are living in neighborhoods with few or no models of good husbands and fathers, of sound healthy relationships between men and women, between husbands and wives. What does it say to our children that so many of the unions that bring children into existence are not sustained? What does this teach them about commitment and trust and love?

## A NOTE ABOUT CAUSATION, BLAME, AND RESPONSIBILITY

The crisis of unwed parenting in the black community is the result of both external and internal factors. It is a function of inadequate economic opportunities as well as government policies that have failed to address, or have exacerbated, the persistent joblessness that confronts large numbers of African American men. There is no doubt that many black men have been seriously disadvantaged by racism, discrimination, and related forces that have made it difficult for them to be good providers and marriage partners (see, for example, Wilson 1996). It is also true that the crisis of unwed parenting is, at least in part, a function of changing attitudes toward sex and marriage in American society in general and in the African American community in particular—changes that tolerate increasingly high rates of out-of-wedlock births and father absence (see, for example, Anderson 1999).

Over the years, in discussing African American unwed parenting in particular, there has been much disagreement about which came first—the external or the internal factors. Much of the argument has been focused on placing blame on racism and on discrimination by those who attribute the problem to external factors, and on individual fathers and mothers and the black community by those who focus on internal factors. But the argument is pointless. By now, it should be clear that external and internal forces are inextricably intertwined and that all these forces must be addressed with equal force and equal urgency.

## THE FOUNDATION OF ALL OUR RIGHTS . . . AND RESPONSIBILITIES

During the Civil War and in the years immediately following the abolition of slavery, the marriage rate among African Americans was high. Slaves, once freed, were eager to exercise what was for them the most fundamental right of freedom—the right to marry and to form families.

Central to the system of slavery was the slaveholder's right to dominion and control over his slaves. Under the law, enslaved Africans were chattel. They had no rights. Every slaveholding state prohibited slaves from entering into legally binding or legally recognized marriages. This obviously did not mean that slave women and men did not have relationships, or even marriages. They were just not legally binding or recognized. In fact, the slave system depended on these so-called contubernial relationships to provide a steady supply of new slaves. Enslaved men and women developed relationships and "jumped the broom" in their own forms of ceremony acknowledging that they, in their own minds, were married. But their unions were not legally recognized and men and women slaves developed loving relationships at their own risk. "Husbands" and "wives" who had committed themselves to each other and thought of themselves as married could be forcibly separated and their children could be taken from them at the slave master's will. In this way, enslaved Africans were denied the most fundamental of human and civil rights—the right to form familial bonds. The denial of that right was the most visible and painful mark of their status as nonpersons. When they were freed, therefore, the right to marry became the most visible sign of their status as persons.

In an enlightening analysis of the significance of marriage in antislavery thought, Peggy Cooper Davis (1997, 9, 35), a legal scholar, concludes that "marriage . . . was the most dramatic and powerful means by which former slaves laid claim to citizenship." Davis continues: "By formalizing family relationships, African Americans consciously claimed the status and responsibilities of spouse, of parent, and of citizen. The formation of legally recognized marriage bonds signified treatment as a human being rather than as chattel—acceptance as people and as members of the political community."

Upon hearing that marriages among African Americans would be solemnized and made legally binding, a black soldier in the midst of the Civil War wrote: "I praise God for this day! I have long been praying for it. The Marriage Covenant is at the foundation of all our rights. In slavery we could not have legalized marriage: now we have it. Let us conduct ourselves worthy of such a blessing—and all the people will respect us—God will bless us, and we shall be established as a people" (Davis 1997, 36).

The soldier was right. The right to marry is the foundation of all our rights. It is the institution that establishes a people. In their book *The War Against Parents,* Sylvia Ann Hewlett and Cornel West (1998, 160) observe that "biologically speaking the link between mother and child is incontrovertible. Fatherhood, in contrast, is inherently uncertain, which is why societies have tried so hard to connect children to their fathers." Hewlett and West remind us that the main cultural vehicle for these sanctions is the institution of marriage, which has served in every known society to hold a man accountable to his children and their mother.

Marriage is the best social institution yet devised for ensuring that children have the benefit of the consistent presence, time, attention, energy, and love of their mothers and their fathers. It is certainly not a perfect institution and it does not guarantee perfect relationships, but it is a society's best assurance of continuity and commitment between men and women and the children they bring into the world.

Strong healthy marriages help build strong healthy families and communities. Children of married parents are more likely to be able to contribute to the larger community because on average they are healthier and better educated and are likely to enjoy greater career success than the children of single parents.

With the high rates of African American children now being born to unmarried mothers and fathers, an overwhelming majority of African American children face dramatically greater risks of negative outcomes in terms of their health and well-being as well as their educational and economic prospects. And they face a greater risk of not being able to establish stable, healthy marriages and families themselves, thereby compromising the health, well-being, and prospects of future generations of African American children.

## THE ROOTS OF MARRIAGE IN
## THE AFRICAN AMERICAN COMMUNITY

In spite of Jim Crow, continuing racism and discrimination, and uncertain economic straits, female-headed households were the exception rather than the rule for African American families for nearly one hundred years, from the period right after the Civil War until the 1960s. How do we explain what appears to have been a rather sudden change in marriage rates for African Americans?

Formerly enslaved African American men and women rushed to get married and form families. But how well they were able to establish their families is a matter of considerable controversy. Some scholars, Herbert Gutman (1976) among them, argue that the men and women who had been enslaved were able against great odds to form "good enough" families. Others, Andrew Billingsley (1992), for example, paint a somewhat rosier picture of a people who emerged from slavery with considerable strengths and little damage to their sense of self-worth and their familial relationships. Others, including E. Franklin Frazier (1939) and Orlando Patterson (1998), argue that slavery left indelible marks visible even today in the lives of African American men and women.

The most reasonable combination of explanations for the dramatic changes in the African American family is that as a result of slavery, the institution of marriage was weakly established in the African American community and therefore more susceptible to cultural, political, and economic changes; and that the emotional legacies of slavery had a greater negative effect on relationships between black men and women than was first thought.

Hewlett and West (1998, 160) note, "In recognition of the problem that fatherhood is enormously important but also somewhat difficult to establish, societies have often created sanctions and imposed stigmas to enforce paternal investment." For fatherhood to take hold and to survive as a vital institution within a society, that society must stand solidly behind it—supporting it with norms, expectations, laws, and resources, over many generations. Societies, in essence, must help men to become good and responsible husbands and fathers.

Starting roughly in the 1960s, however, all across the world the most wealthy and technologically advanced societies began abandoning the work of helping men become good husbands and fathers. As Western countries became increasingly driven by an emphasis on personal freedom and self-fulfillment and a deemphasis on obligation, their societal commitment to establishing and maintaining the father-child bond decreased dramatically (see Morehouse Research Institute and Institute for American Values 1999, 9). Not surprisingly, given the fragility of the father-child bond and the decreasing commitment to enforcing the norms that keep fathers committed to children, many fathers throughout the Western world began disengaging from their children and their families.

All American men were affected to one degree or another by these profound global cultural shifts. For African American men, however, the effects of these changes were exacerbated by worsening economic and social conditions (see Morehouse Research Institute and Institute for American Values 1999, 10–12). They were also aggravated by the persistent legacies of slavery and racism.

The sociologist Orlando Patterson (1998, 27) has offered a provocative, important, and timely reminder of the legacy of slavery and its effects on the institutions of fatherhood and marriage in black America. He observes that slavery was "most virulent in its devastation of the roles of father and husband." For the Africans brought to America and enslaved, the institution of fatherhood never had the backing—let alone the solid backing—of the society in which they were enslaved. Conditions for Africans in the United States provided exactly the opposite of what is required to establish and preserve the fragile bond between father and child. By law, the male slave could not fully carry out the duties of husband and father. The institution of slavery created a subculture where all the societal norms, mores, expectations, laws, and the force of government, instead of enforcing paternal investment, enforced paternal disinvestment. Instead of teaching enslaved men to provide for and to be responsible for their offspring, slavery taught them not to be responsible, not to provide.

The institution of chattel slavery in the United States intentionally separated procreation by men from the capacity to provide for their children and their children's mothers. The critical link between reproductive behavior and the ability and responsibility to provide for one's offspring was forcibly severed over the course of nearly three centuries of slavery.

Moreover, the practices of slaveholders in the United States had a devastating effect on relationships between black men and women. Slavery led to profound distrust in gender relationships: "In the absence of any legally recognized marriage rights in his partner; and in the presence of both predatory Euro-American men, who could rape or otherwise sexually manipulate slave women with impunity, and a large minority of other young, unattached slave men . . . the male slave was placed in an impossible situation, one bound to reduce him to a state of chronic jealousy and insecurity about women" (Patterson 1998, 35).

Slaveholders also created conditions in which most black women could not count on their men. According to Brenda Lane Richardson and Brenda Wade (1999, 42–43),

> In the infamous and at the time widely distributed, Lynch letter, Willie Lynch, a slave owner in the West Indies, advocated mind control techniques. He recommended torturing and humiliating a black man in front of his wife and children and stripping him naked and tying each of his ankles to wild horses who pulled in opposite directions. Lynch believed punishments such as this reinforced the belief in black women that their men could not protect them. These methods, Lynch advised, would create an atmosphere in which: "You've got a nigger woman out front and the nigger man behind and scared."

These conditions of slavery had a brutal effect on men, women, and children, and in the view of a growing number of scholars and commentators, they established damaging patterns that have been reproduced from one generation to another, surviving in many families to this day (Grier and Cobbs 1968; hooks 1993; Wyatt 1997; Patterson 1998; Richardson and Wade 1999; Poussaint and Alexander 2000).

In examining the legacy of emotions and feelings that developed from slavery through Jim Crow, Richardson and Wade (1999, xx) argue that "a culture born of the slavery experience has been passed from generation to generation." Their work reminds us that it has only been a few generations since the official end of slavery and less than forty years since the Civil Rights Act of 1964 put a formal end to Jim Crow, which continued many of the dehumanizing practices that had begun in slavery. They show how slavery planted within enslaved men and women seeds of inferiority, self-hatred, and shame—seeds that in far too many families were passed on through generations. They observe that "our unknown great-great-grandparents' shame lives on in our collective memory. Our history didn't just happen to a group of anonymous people. These people were our ancestors, and in many respects, they are a part of us" (Richardson and Wade 1999, xix–xx).

In the understandable rush to marry and to establish families after the Civil War, African Americans never took the necessary time to heal the deep wounds that had been inflicted by slavery and passed down from one generation to the next. Nor did the African American community take the necessary time to heal from the brutalities and indignities of Jim Crow. Richardson and Wade (1999, 44–45) demonstrate convincingly how certain damaging beliefs and attitudes about black men have been passed down to many black women—beliefs such as "if we had to depend on your daddy, we'd be on the street," and "that man only wants one thing." These beliefs and attitudes, established in slavery and fanned by embers of continuing racism and economic discrimination, make it difficult for many black men and women to establish trusting, loving, healthy relationships and marriages today.

This analysis of the relationship between slavery and racism and African American fatherhood and marriage helps to explain why African American marriages were especially vulnerable to changes in norms and economic conditions. It also makes all the more heroic the many black men and women throughout African American history who, with all the forces arrayed against them, nevertheless assumed and fulfilled their responsibilities to each other and to their children. The creation of so many strong African American families against these odds shows the awesome power of the African American spirit to "make a way out of no way," to overcome even the most apparently insurmountable challenges. It is a story that offers great hope that we can—and that we will—overcome the present crisis of father absence in the African American community, and rebuild the institution of marriage—this time with deeper, stronger, healthier roots.

## REFERENCES

Anderson, Elijah. 1999. *Code of the Street: Decency, Violence, and the Moral Life of the Inner City*. New York: Norton.

Billingsley, Andrew. 1992. *Climbing Jacob's Ladder: The Enduring Legacy of African American Families*. New York: Simon & Schuster.

Coalition for Marriage, Family and Couples Education. 2000. *The Marriage Movement: A Statement of Principles*. Statement prepared in cooperation with the Religion, Culture and Family Project, University of Chicago. New York: Institute for American Values.

Daly, Martin, and Margo Wilson. 1996. "Evolutionary Psychology and Mental Conflict: The Relevance of Stepchildren." In *Sex, Power, Conflict: Evolutionary and Feminist Perspectives*, edited by David M. Buss and Neil Malamuile. New York: Oxford University Press.

Davis, Peggy Cooper. 1997. *Neglected Stories: The Constitution and Family Values*. New York: Hill & Wang.

Dupree, Allen, and Wendell Primus. 2001. "Declining Share of Children Lived with Single Mothers in the Late 1990's." Report. Washington: Center on Budget and Policy Priorities.

Frazier, E. Franklin. 1939. *The Negro Family in the United States*. Chicago, University of Chicago Press.

Grier, William, and Price Cobbs. 1968. *Black Rage*. New York: Bantam Books.

Gutman, Herbert G. 1976. *The Black Family in Slavery and Freedom, 1750–1925*. New York: Vintage Books.

Harper, Cynthia C., and Sara S. McLanahan. 1998. "Father Absence and Youth Incarceration." Paper presented to the annual meeting of the American Sociological Association. San Francisco (August).

Hewlett, Sylvia Ann, and Cornel West. 1998. *The War Against Parents: What We Can Do for American's Beleaguered Moms and Dads*. Boston: Houghton Mifflin.

hooks, bell. 1993. *Sisters of Yam: Black Women and Self-Recovery*. Boston: South End Press.

McLanahan, Sara, and Gary Sandefur. 1994. *Growing Up with a Single Parent: What Hurts, What Helps*. Cambridge, Mass.: Harvard University Press.

Morehouse Research Institute and Institute for American Values. 1999. *Turning the Corner on Father Absence in Black America*. A Statement from the Morehouse Conference on African American Fathers. Atlanta: Morehouse Research Institute and Institute for American Values.

Ooms, Theodora. 1998. *Toward More Perfect Unions: Putting Marriage on the Public Agenda.* Washington, D.C.: Family Impact Seminar.

Patterson, Orlando. 1998. *Rituals of Blood: Consequences of Slavery in Two American Centuries.* Washington, D.C.: Civitas.

Poussaint, Alvin F., and Amy Alexander. 2000. *Lay My Burden Down: Unraveling Suicide and the Mental Health Crisis Among African Americans.* Boston: Beacon Press.

Powell, Kevin. *Keepin' It Real.* 1997. New York: Ballantine.

Richardson, Brenda Lane, and Brenda Wade. 1999. *What Mamma Couldn't Tell Us About Love: Healing the Emotional Legacy of Racism by Celebrating Our Light.* New York: Perennial.

Waite, Linda J., and Maggie Gallagher. 2000. *The Case for Marriage: Why Married People are Happier, Healthier, and Better Off Financially.* New York: Doubleday.

Wilson, William Julius. 1996. *When Work Disappears: The World of the New Urban Poor.* New York: Knopf.

Wyatt, Gail Elizabeth. 1997. *Stolen Women: Reclaiming Our Sexuality, Taking Back Our Lives.* New York: John Wiley.

# Conclusions

OBIE CLAYTON, RONALD B. MINCY, AND DAVID BLANKENHORN

In the summer of 2001, a series of independent reports based largely on new data from the 2000 Census, all pointed toward a remarkable social and demographic fact. After at least four decades of steadily getting weaker, the black family today seems to be getting stronger.

Paralleling positive developments in family structure, white America may currently be poised to follow black America when it comes to the turnaround in family structure. The proportion of all U.S. families with children under age eighteen that are headed by married couples reached an all-time low in the mid-1990s—about 72.9 percent in 1996 and 72.4 percent in 1997—but since then has stabilized. The figure for 2000 is 73 percent (U.S. Bureau of the Census 2001a).

Similarly, the proportion of all U.S. children living in two-parent homes reached an all-time low in the mid-1990s, but since then has stabilized. In fact, the proportion of children in two-parent homes increased from 68 percent in 1999 to 69.1 percent in 2000 (U.S. Bureau of the Census 2001b, F10A–F).

A study that looked only at white, non-Hispanic children finds that the proportion of these children living with two married parents stopped its downward descent during the late 1990s, and even increased slightly from 1999 to 2000, rising from 77.3 to 78.2 percent (Dupree and Primus 2001). Another study finds that, among all U.S. children, the proportion living with their two biological or adoptive parents increased by 1.2 percent from 1997 to 1999, while during the same period the proportion living in stepfamilies (or blended families) decreased by 0.1 percentage point and the proportion living in single-parent homes decreased by 2 percentage points. (The study finds that in 1999 about 64 percent of all U.S. children lived with their two biological or adoptive parents, while about 25 percent lived with one parent and about 8 percent lived in a stepfamily or blended family.) Among low-income children, the decline in the proportion living in single-parent homes was even more pronounced, dropping from 44 percent in 1997 to 41 percent in 1999 (Vandivere, Moore, and Zaslow 2001). Unpublished data from this study show that, among all U.S. children, the proportion residing with their own two married biological or adoptive parents remained roughly constant from 1997 (60.3 percent) to 1999 (60.7 percent).

Drawing on many of the analyses offered by the contributors to this volume, here is our first conclusion: steadily increasing the proportion over the next ten years of black children who are residing with their responsible, loving fathers is both necessary and possible. This reintegration of nurturing black fathers into the homes and therefore the lives of their children is the prime goal, the umbrella priority, under which all the others fit.

This brings us to our second conclusion: because marriage is a vital support for effective fatherhood, and because marriage on average provides the optimal environment for healthy child development, a major priority for black America and for the society as a whole should be to steadily increase the proportion of children growing up in two-biological-parent, married-couple homes. The entire priority of fathers' residency with children leads to the question of the father-mother relationship, which in turn of course leads to the question of marriage. The issue of marriage is complex and difficult, as is evidenced by the breadth of opinion on the issue in the marriage and family literature. On one end of the philosophical spectrum is the belief that promoting married fatherhood should be the overriding ethic and goal of a modern fatherhood movement. On the other end of the spectrum is the belief that today's fatherhood leaders, programs, and messages should be strictly neutral, or nonjudgmental, on the question of marriage.

The three editors of this volume are themselves not entirely in agreement regarding the exact role of marriage in the renewal of black (and American) fatherhood. But we *are* agreed that marriage matters; that it is quite unlikely that we as a society will be able to turn the corner on father absence while simultaneously witnessing and permitting the further disintegration of marriage; and that therefore, as a general rule, bringing back the fathers and strengthening marriage are goals that stand best when they stand together.

Let us stress briefly some of the economic aspects of the marriage challenge. As Ronald Mincy and Hillard Pouncy's and also Maggie

Gallagher's contribution to this volume emphasize, marriage is in part a wealth-producing institution. Married people earn, invest, and save more than unmarried people. These findings cannot be explained away by the likelihood that economically successful people are also more likely to marry. Nor does cohabitation generate economic gains equivalent to those generated by marriage. Marriage itself changes behavior in ways that tend to make people financially better off (see Waite and Gallagher 2000).

As mentioned previously, marriage is in large part an economic partnership in which two people pool their resources, support one another's lives and careers, draw upon one another's social and family networks, compensate for one another's weaknesses, share tasks in an efficient way, and work cooperatively toward the goal of financial success. There are many ways to jump into the middle or upper class, of course, from winning the lottery to starting a successful business. But for most people, an essential foundation for long-term economic achievement is a stable marriage.

These economic facts pose a special challenge to African Americans. Currently, by age thirty, about 80 percent of white women but only 45 percent of black women have ever married (Bachrach, Hindin, and Thomson 2000, 3). About 70 percent of all black children today are born to never-married mothers (McLanahan et al. 2000). Forget for a moment about child development, social expectations, or "family values." Just follow where the money is likely to go. Marriage is a primary gateway to economic success. Accordingly, for an entire rising generation of young African Americans, including the growing numbers who will have attended college, the absence of a stable marriage may be the single most important barrier keeping them from entering the middle and upper classes. For this and other reasons, giving up on marriage, even while pursuing second-best solutions, is ultimately a form of defeatism, the economic equivalent of sitting at the back of the bus.

Continuing progress on this issue may be possible. For example, research by Sara McLanahan of Princeton and her colleagues finds that among low-income black single mothers, almost half are living with the father at the time of the birth. A substantial majority of these couples say that they are romantically involved, and that they either hope or plan to get married (McLanahan et al. 2000; Waller 2001, 457–84; Garfinkel et al. 2000, 277–301). This is good news. This research shows, among other things, that the desire for a stable marriage is not a "white" value. On the contrary, marriage is a nearly universal human aspiration, even in communities where marriage as an institution has been severely weakened.

Most of these inner-city, low-income couples do not marry. But why? Could we help at least some of them to achieve their goal of a good marriage? Currently we do almost nothing to assist these people achieve successful marriages. What if, starting soon, whenever these young parents come into contact with a social worker or public agency, they are given the option of being referred to a local church or civic group that will help them to develop the skills and resources necessary for a successful marriage?

Here is our third conclusion: although new government policies cannot by themselves cause a renewal of black (and American) fatherhood, policy reforms can and, we believe, must play an important role in helping to support fathers and fatherhood, especially in fragile families. A laissez-faire approach—the less government, the better—is, at least with respect to the issue of father absence, fundamentally inappropriate.

Support for this idea comes from a 2000 study by the Manpower Demonstration Research Corporation, which found that the state of Minnesota's welfare reform program, called the Minnesota Family Investment Program, has led to higher marriage rates, more marital stability, and lower divorce rates among the program's participants. Why? No definitive answers have emerged, but the Minnesota program combined a strong emphasis on work with a generous set of wage supplements and other financial benefits (Knox, Miller, and Gennetian 2000). These encouraging family and fatherhood results seem to have come not from government's doing and spending less, but from government's doing and spending more—combined with different and better. The lesson seems to be that jump-starts in financial security can also foster more and better marriages, which in turn foster financial success. Liberals, who often emphasize economic justice, and conservatives, who often emphasize the traditional family, may be able to join forces in support of this approach.

Similarly, several bills introduced in the U.S. Congress in 2000 and 2001, most with bipartisan sponsorship and support, would authorize significant increases in federal funding for community-based fatherhood programs aimed at reducing the prevalence of father absence in the United States, particularly in our poorest communities, and at incorporating a recognition of the importance of marriage. These efforts are relatively new and therefore largely untested, but they are promising and worthy of support.

Here is our final conclusion: contemporary U.S. father absence is less a black crisis than an American crisis, one that affects the entire society. Stemming primarily from broad societal trends, not subcultural, racial, or ethnic trends, the crisis of black fathers, though urgent in its own right and deserving of special attention from policy makers, cannot be separated, analytically or prescriptively, from the broader crisis of U.S. fathers, which cuts across all lines of race and class. The fatherhood crisis we face in the United States is essentially *societal*, not racial (although it has racial aspects and implications). Neither is it a correlate of economic status (although it has clear economic dimensions). For this reason, our response to the crisis must also be *societal* in nature. In the final analysis, fatherlessness is not a "them" problem. It's an "us" problem.

## REFERENCES

Bachrach, Christine, Michelle J. Hindin, and Elizabeth Thomson. 2000. "The Changing Shape of Ties That Bind: An Overview and Synthesis." In *The Ties That Bind: Perspective on Marriage and Cohabitation*, edited by Linda J. Waite. New York: Aldine de Gruyter.

Dupree, Allen, and Wendell Primus. 2001. *Declining Share of Children Lived with Single Mothers in the Late 1990s*. Washington, D.C.: Center on Budget and Policy Priorities (June).

Franklin, Donna L. 1997. *Ensuring Inequality: The Structural Transformation of the African-American Family*. New York: Oxford University Press.

Garfinkel, Irwin, Sara S. McLanahan, Marta Tienda, and Jeanne Brooks-Gunn. 2000. "Fragile Families and Welfare Reform: An Introduction." *Child and Youth Service Review* 23(4–5): 277–301.

Knox, Virginia, Cynthia Miller, and Lisa A. Gennetian. 2000. *Reforming Welfare and Rewarding Work: A Summary of the Final Report on the Minnesota Family Investment Program*. New York: Manpower Demonstration Research Corporation.

McLanahan, Sara, Irwin Garfinkel, Nancy Reichman, and Julien Teitler. 2000. "Unwed Parents or Fragile Families? Implications for Welfare and Child Support Policy" Working paper no. 00–04. Princeton, N.J.: Center for Research on Child Wellbeing.

U.S. Bureau of the Census. 2001a. "Families, by Presence of Own Children Under 18: 1950 to Present." Current Population Reports, series P20-537: table FM-1.

————. 2001b. "Living Arrangements of Children Under 18 Years Old: 1960 to Present." Current Population Reports, series P20-537: table CH-1.

Vandivere, Sharon, Kristen Anderson Moore, and Martha Zaslow. 2001. *Children's Family Environments: Findings from the National Survey of America's Families.* Washington, D.C.: Urban Institute.

Waite, Linda J., and Maggie Gallagher. 2000. *The Case for Marriage: Why Married People Are Happier, Healthier, and Better Off Financially.* New York: Doubleday.

Waller, Maureen R. 2001. "High Hopes: Unwed Parents' Expectations About Marriage." *Children and Youth Service Review* 23(6–7): 457–87.

# INDEX

Numbers in **boldface** refer to figures and tables.